THE
SAN FRANCISCO
DOODLER
MURDERS

THE
SAN FRANCISCO
DOODLER
MURDERS

KATE ZALIZNOCK

THE
History
PRESS

Published by The History Press
Charleston, SC
www.historypress.com

Front cover: *Aerial of the Cliff House*, Cara Moore, 1974. *Courtesy of the artist.*
Back cover: *Balloons Being Released from Roofs at Castro St. Fair*, 1976. *Courtesy of the San Francisco Public Library.*

First published 2022

Manufactured in the United States

ISBN 9781467149877

Library of Congress Control Number: 2022937933

For my mother, Mary, who taught me how to wonder,
and for Dr. Chapman Greer, who taught me how to write.

But what if it prove that I am no harper?
That I lied for your love most monstrously?

—Peter S. Beagle

CONTENTS

CONTENTS

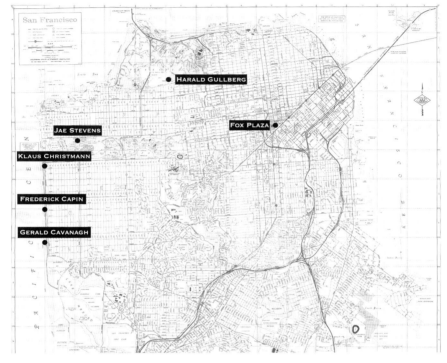

HARALD GULLBERG

JAE STEVENS

KLAUS CHRISTMANN

FREDERICK CAPIN

GERALD CAVANAGH

FOX PLAZA

Map by Kate Zaliznock.

PROLOGUE

To write a book about an unsolved case is not an easy thing, yet a story unfinished should not be a story untold. When dealing with a cold case from the 1970s, the clock seems to tick at a faster speed. Justice feels like the last drop of water in a depthless well. Time becomes a thief in the night; death comes for surviving witnesses, victims' loved ones, original investigating officers. Archives are lost; journalists' notes vanish into the ether. The California Public Records Act becomes the bane of your existence.

Yet, in these cases, the possibilities outweigh the setbacks—it could take just one person, one piece of evidence, one dot to connect all the rest. For decades, justice has eluded the victims of a calculated killer. Memories fade, time marches on, yet truth stains what it touches, marking the past with its presence.

Someone, somewhere, knows something.

CALIFORNIA FULLY BLOSSOMED AS a notoriously fertile breeding ground for serial killers in the 1970s. These murderers have been studied for decades by law enforcement, behavioral scientists, psychiatrists, psychologists, and the general public at large.

Since DNA testing was first used to solve a crime in 1986, more serial killers have emerged from the shadows. Murders once considered random acts were suddenly connected in strings of brutal homicides committed by

Castro Theatre, San Francisco. *Photo by Carol Highsmith. Courtesy of Library of Congress.*

the same individual. How many of these career killers were out there? It's a question every major jurisdiction in California has asked itself.

In San Francisco, one killer would step out into the night and claim a minimum of five confirmed victims, all within the city's gay scene. At the time, a serial killer was the least of the LGBTQ community's worries; almost nightly, its members were harassed or assaulted on the streets of the Castro, SoMa, and Tenderloin districts.

The violence was omnipresent, yet so was the LGBTQ rights movement. The decade began with the first Pride Parade, on June 28, 1970, in New York City. San Francisco soon adopted the celebration, calling it the Gay Freedom Parade. Harvey Milk moved to San Francisco in 1972 and ran for city supervisor the following year.

In 1973, the American Psychiatric Association removed homosexuality as a mental disorder from the third edition of its *Diagnostic and Statistical Manual*, considered to be the Bible of psychologists and psychiatrists. By 1975, politicians such as Dianne Feinstein were actively campaigning against the discrimination experienced by the LGBTQ community. The San Francisco

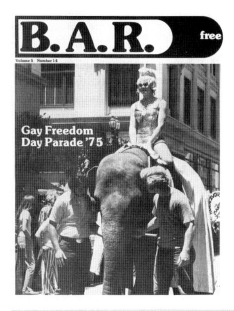

This page: *Bay Area Reporter.*

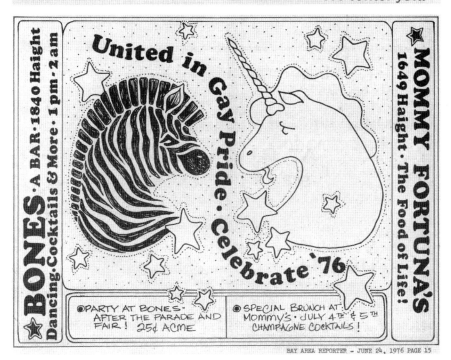

Police Department was rightly confronted for its failure to protect LGBTQ citizens; it would spend much of the decade attempting to chip away at the deeply embedded discriminatory practices within the institution.

The Castro nightlife flourished, filled to the brim with bars and restaurants catering to the LGBTQ community. Numerous businesses built their success on providing a safe LGBTQ space. There would be one man who hunted within these circles—a friendly face with a warm smile and welcoming eyes. Under the glow of neon lights, through streets still bustling well past midnight, this man lured his prey into the dark to their deaths.

This killer's victims would barely get any press coverage—sometimes just a line or two that flatly announced the discovery of their bodies. As the death toll rose, the connection between the murderer and San Francisco's gay nightlife scene became apparent to law enforcement. The investigation was quickly hindered by the practically nonexistent relationship between the LGBTQ community and the San Francisco Police Department. Unlike in cases involving straight victims, there was a long, dark history of discrimination within not only the police department but society itself. Homophobia came to play the role of the killer's accomplice, his most trusted co-conspirator—the invisible shield that guarded his identity.

A combination of advanced technology and cultural progress increases the possibility of a resolution in the case of the Doodler Murders. Though files have yellowed, buried beneath the ever-increasing caseload of the San Francisco Police Department's homicide unit, the lives of the Doodler's victims have not been forgotten by their precious few loved ones who remain. The public, who once ignored the staggering number of LGBTQ homicides in the city, still has the chance to reach back into the depths of time to pull a killer from the shadows.

Chapter 1

DEAD IN THE WATER

The sea's edge at Ocean Beach can be a deceptively murderous swirl. Long has it drawn many a victim into its seemingly docile waves with their soft-crumbling crests, invitingly low and unassuming. Over the years, numerous men, women, and children have wandered out for a quick dip in the frigid waters, never to be seen again. This is the deadliest place to swim in all of California's Bay Area. The year 1974 would also mark it as a hunting ground for one of the most lethal serial killers in the entirety of San Francisco's history.

The night of January 27, 1974, was cold, dark, and foggy. The soft sand hardened as two men walked toward the shoreline, finally touching the water. Despite its forty-degree weather, Ocean Beach was once again up and running as a favored lovers' lane for San Francisco's gay community. Just a few weeks prior, the city had experienced an extreme cold spell; despite a deep chill that still hung in the air, the weather had vastly improved. It was here where Gerald Earl Cavanagh strolled down to the sea's edge alongside his killer.

It would have taken them a few minutes to make their way over the rolling dunes to the frothing sea. It's hard to believe that in those moments, Gerald didn't sense anything amiss. When the coy chatter ceased, perhaps he turned away from the killer, so as to not convey concern.

The stabbing was fueled by rage and not mere efficiency, the killer purging himself of a deep-seated hatred, if only for a moment. Gerald had no time to fight back after he was struck multiple times on the right side of his head;

The Cliff House, overlooking Ocean Beach. *Photo by Carol Highsmith. Courtesy of Library of Congress.*

a gash on his left pinky finger was later noted by the coroner as his only defense wound. When the murderer finished, he made his escape. Perhaps hurriedly, perhaps not; either way, the deepening sand would have slowed him, extending the time between the killing and the leaving—time spent with a racing mind and a ticking clock.

At 1:25 a.m., the phone rang at the San Francisco Police Department. A voice came on the line, measured but with an undercurrent of distress. The person reported seeing Gerald's body on the beach but declined to provide a name or contact information. At 1:57 a.m., the coroner was notified, after Officer Gunter and Sergeant Mahoney responded to the scene to find Gerald dead—blood-soaked and nearly pulled out to sea.

As he took his last breaths, Gerald looked upward at the sky. The sixteen stab wounds took his life quickly, but not before he realized his fate. There was no bullet to the head, no rapid-fire execution to prevent this. Gerald was perfectly sober; the sharp realization that he was dying was not dulled by the effects of drugs or alcohol—his shock, confusion, and panic had time to register before his life ended.

Aerial view of Ocean Beach and Great Highway. *Photo by Alex Bierwagen. Courtesy of Unsplash.*

It is tragically poetic that Gerald's last name is misspelled throughout the bits and pieces of available research. Because he was a closeted gay man, his murder was swiftly narrated by the public as a tale of two men sneaking away for discreet sex—thrill-seeking deviants already embroiled in the underbelly of society. Was it such a stretch to think this encounter could go wrong? Wasn't it obvious? A staggering number of gay men had to die before this case—and many others—would get a deeper look.

OCEAN BEACH IS THE perfect opposite of the lively, neon-lit, bustling hub of the Castro's nightlife, where the LGBTQ community openly thrived. To drive to Ocean Beach from the Castro, one follows the long, horizontal stretch of Golden Gate Park until its dead end at Great Highway, which runs parallel to the Pacific Ocean. On a clear day, spectacular sunsets backlight the Farallon Islands—barren, jutting rock formations that rise up out of the sea and serve as one of the most populous migration points in the world for great white sharks. Most nights, though, the fog rolls in and saturates the air, obscuring Great Highway's dotted streetlights and transforming them into eerie orbs. In the dark, it is not a particularly inviting place; on a cold, foggy night, it can be downright haunting.

It is unclear where exactly Gerald met his killer, but legend would later tell he was possibly in a Castro bar or restaurant during the late evening hours of January 26, 1974. In this story, the killer sat a measured distance from him, but close enough to view the details of Gerald's features: the small scar on his forehead, the thinning gray hair swept over patches of baldness, his blue eyes. The killer bent over a scrap of paper and went to work. With a skilled hand, he drew Gerald's face, smoothing the forty-nine-year-old's aged appearance and editing him into an idealized version of himself—an accurate but improved depiction. The killer's demeanor was confident yet unassuming; he charmed and disarmed the unmarried, middle-aged mattress factory worker and Army veteran within minutes. At barely twenty years old, the killer flattered Gerald with his interest. The tangible souvenir he produced was a successful lure.

POLICE LATER DUBBED GERALD's killer "the Doodler," an oddball name for an outlier killer and not one befitting the terror he unleashed on San Francisco's gay community. Whereas many serial killers have searing words in their nicknames, like "slasher," "ripper," "lethal" and, of course, "killer," police calling Gerald's murderer the Doodler seems to add a whimsical touch to this savage killing, as though he was some cartoon character fumbling through the night.

There are at least four other known victims in the Doodler murder series and all have several key points of similarity. All were white, gay men who were stabbed to death in relatively remote locations in San Francisco. All of these murders could have, should have, been solved back in the 1970s, but none were. The reason why is heartbreaking.

The relationship between the gay community and the police was marked by suspicious tension. Beat cops had turned their title into a pun and often harassed men in the Castro. One division of the SFPD came to develop a particularly strained dynamic with LGBTQ citizens: the homicide unit.

ROTEA GILFORD WOULD BECOME a legend. As the first Black police inspector, who rose to be the first Black member of the homicide unit, "Gil," as he came to be known among the ranks, knew his legacy was just as important as the impact he could have on San Francisco while he was alive. When the Doodler Murders began, Gilford and his partner, Prentice Earl Sanders, were in the throes of one of the most controversial cases San Francisco had ever seen. The Zebra Murders were a series of brutal, targeted killings of an assortment of white people by radical Black members of the self-titled Death Angels group. In what were also known as the .32-Caliber Killings, victims were randomly selected by a roaming group of men who gunned down targets in the streets or—in two cases—employed machetes and knives. As the death toll rose to twenty-six, Gilford and Sanders were feeling the pressure from the public, the media, and their fellow officers to solve the case. The two worked under the direction of lead investigators Gus Coreris and John Fotinos.

Gilford was no stranger to walking the line between volatile cultural disputes. Nicknamed "Officer Smiley" by Fillmore residents who frequently encountered him during his first beat, he was well known to be exceptionally adept at disarming even the most aggressive of characters and was able to de-escalate a number of situations. His skills would prove valuable in solving the Zebra killings and, later, investigating the Doodler Murders as well.

Gilford's early life was earmarked by successes in football, a sport that came to serve as a living metaphor for his ingrained values well after his retirement. He dedicated his life to mentoring and serving vulnerable youths by introducing them to the sport as a way of learning responsibility, accountability, and a sense of future opportunity. While in the SFPD's homicide unit, he employed many of these same principles.

Officer Rotea Gilford. *Courtesy of the SFPD.*

When it came to public relations, Gilford was anything but run-of-the-mill. He spoke relatively freely, a straight shooter with the media who cared more about connecting with the community than prioritizing political correctness. He forged numerous relationships within the Black community, and eventually, he came to be known for his work with the LGBTQ community as well. For many, he would come to represent the best the police force had to offer.

Gilford's style of work was textbook "community policing," well before the term was on the books. He never wavered from his conviction that for law enforcement to be successful, the police force would need to be representative of the community it served. The utter lack of Black officers in the SFPD was directly linked to the stark divide between cops and community; racism ran deep and only served to further hinder investigations and crime prevention.

Prentice Earl Sanders partnered with Gilford in 1971. Sanders held a deep regard for Gilford's achievements, both within the SFPD and as a member of the Black community. Both Sanders and Gilford had not only excelled in their training and performance but also did so under the enormous weight of racism, simultaneously blatant and unassuming. Sanders had grown up in Texas, and as he put it to writer Bennett Cohen,

> *Racism in San Francisco wasn't like down South. There wasn't some scowling cracker on the other end of the whip. In San Francisco, racism came at you with a smile. Like they were doing you a favor when they told you that they didn't have any jobs open after you'd seen a half dozen white guys fill out applications, or that you couldn't buy a house when they'd just sold one to a white who made less money. Despite all that, something about San Francisco seemed to hold the promise of opportunity.*

Sanders was ten years younger than Gilford and stood in awe of his accomplishments, how he'd navigated a police force that had for decades been tightly controlled by Irish American top brass—many of whom had no interest in diversifying the ranks. Gilford manifested his advocacy for fellow Black members of the SFPD through the creation of a union called Officers for Justice, which sued the SFPD for discrimination and, in 1979, earned a consent decree requiring the SFPD to improve its hiring and promotional practices.

Gilford and Sanders spent the night Gerald was killed deep in the Zebra Murders investigation; they regularly worked twenty-four-hour shifts on the

Prentice Earl Sanders in 1968.
Courtesy of the SFPD.

case. The city was being terrorized, and as Black investigators, they were facing racist scrutiny from those who felt the detectives would not properly investigate the case out of loyalty to the Black community. The pressure to solve the Zebra case didn't only come from the outside. This was a deeply personal case to Gilford and Sanders, for the Zebra killers represented all the two officers had fought against for their entire careers. Not only were these murders racially motivated, but they were also aiming to be a shot through the heart of the Civil Rights Movement. Gilford and Sanders would never stand for it—not on their watch.

SAN FRANCISCO CULTURE IN the 1970s was a hodgepodge of progressive policy, burnout from 1967's Summer of Love, a strengthened Civil Rights Movement, and conservative outrage. That the LGBTQ community was discriminated against did not go unnoticed by the two detectives. The targeting of gay men and LGBTQ establishments was completely at odds with Gilford's vision of community policing. It buttressed the very obstacles he and Sanders faced while later investigating the Doodler.

The gay community's tight-lipped relationship with law enforcement was not just strategic; at times, staying at a distance was essential in order to protect lives and welfare. LGBTQ-friendly establishments were frequently raided, with patrons lined up for arrest and public humiliation. The benefits of cooperation with the police were mostly few and far between. It would turn out that not even widespread bloodshed could open the floodgates of mutual participation in solving the case. The reality was, the stakes were just too high.

On January 28, Gerald's body was being processed by the coroner, and Gilford and Sanders started their day by continuing the Zebra investigation. At that time, there hadn't been a Zebra shooting in over a month, and the partners decided they might finally be able to have a night off. A few hours later, on the twenty-ninth of January, the deadliest night of the Zebra Murder series began. Before Gerald's body was released from the coroner on January 30, Gilford and Sanders were even deeper into a seemingly never-ending search for the Zebra killers.

To describe Gilford and Sanders's plates as full would be almost comical—it would be far more accurate to say the plates were full, the table was full, the room was full, the house was full...all of it. It didn't help that Gilford was still mending from a divorce the year prior, and he often leaned on Sanders as a friend—Sanders regarded that as an honor, not a duty. The time Sanders spent between his cases and his after-hours hangouts with Gilford accumulated enough for Sanders to feel how his absence from home affected his family. He knew, though—felt it in his bones—that pursuing justice for all of these victims, from the Zebra killings to the Doodler Murders, wasn't something he could back down from.

Chapter 2

A STAR IS DEAD

T he second victim of the Doodler was twenty-seven-year-old Joseph "Jae" Stevens, who was found shortly after his death near Spreckels Lake in Golden Gate Park on June 25, 1974. An on/off San Francisco resident, Jae was dazzling and bubbly; he drew everyone in with his warm personality and sparkling humor. A full-page obituary featured in *Drag Magazine* reflects on how he was

> *certainly one of the most loved performers by his peers in San Francisco. To work with him was a joy and those of us who were privileged to know him will always remember his great ability to find humor in any situation, his genuine warmth and caring of everyone around him and his total lack of temperament.…In those brief 27 years, he brought a lot of love to the people around him. The world will go on turning but it is now minus one beautiful, caring human being.*

Jae had long brown hair and, like Gerald, blue eyes. At five feet, ten inches and 145 pounds, there was an elegance about him—which cemented his reputation as a star-studded performer. His flair for fashion didn't hurt, either. When he last left home, he selected blue pants and a patterned shirt. If he carried anything else on his person, it was never found.

At some point during the night of June 24, Jae encountered his killer. The frequent center-stage entertainer had no lack of admirers throughout the LGBTQ community—that the murderer stood out from a crowd serves as further evidence of a startling mastery of deception.

This page and opposite: Joseph "Jae" Stevens. *Courtesy of Melissa Honrath.*

The pair found themselves near Spreckels Lake, located on the north side of Golden Gate Park parallel to Fulton Street. During the day, parkgoers stroll past the serene spot, often stopping to feed the sizeable raft of ducks that has acquired permanent residence on the lake. As in most of Golden Gate Park, lush trees surround the area and hide away visitors from the main road that lies just feet away.

Like Ocean Beach, Spreckels Lake and many other Golden Gate Park locations served as common nighttime rendezvous places for gay partners looking for a discreet hookup location. Jae's car was later found parked nearby; it is possible he had unwittingly chauffeured his killer to his own murder scene.

The lack of defense wounds on Jae's hands indicates he, like Gerald, had his back turned to the killer before the knife's first strike. A C-shaped abrasion below his right eye likely indicated an initial blow to the ground, but the coroner could not be sure. Either way, what followed was a rapid succession of stabbings to the back and chest, with severe punctures to both lungs. Jae, like Gerald, was found in a supine position, and his blood alcohol level indicated he had consumed no more than one drink on the night he was killed.

At around five o'clock in the morning, shortly after Jae's murder, his car was seen in Hayward, approximately an hour-long drive away from where his body lay, still undiscovered. The driver was roaming a spot in town that had recently been rife with rape attacks when a passing deputy attempted to pull him over. Suddenly, the car took off, and a high-speed chase followed.

When the driver of Jae's car finally lost control and drove into a house, the officer was able to obtain a description: a white man with blond, shoulder-length hair.

As of 2022, the Hayward Police Department maintains that any records of the car chase incident or subsequent arrests have either been lost or, much more likely, destroyed. The San Francisco Police Department included the report in their investigation of Jae's murder, however.

MARY MELISSA STEVENS, NOW Melissa Honrath, remembers her brother Jae as her best friend. She and Jae would stage plays together in the family's basement in Concord, California—scenes that eventually grew into a touring comedy show. She describes Jae—or Joe, as he called himself at home—as the kind and gentle soul numerous others would attest to as well, always welcoming his loved ones with a hug and a smile.

When it comes to Jae's gender identity, Melissa says, "If my brother were to be labeled right now, he would definitely be transgender." As Jae still referred to himself as he/him within the LGBTQ community at the time of his death, this book continues to do so, as does Melissa. That Jae did not live long enough to make his own decision on such a personal subject as gender identity is yet one of an incalculable number of consequences of the killer's crimes. It's notable that when Jae and Melissa played together as small children, he asked that she call him Carolyn.

Jae was a bright light in his family.

So much fun. He was so much fun. We did a lot of talent shows together and acting together. My parents, bless their hearts, gave us the run of the garage. So we had neighborhood shows, and we had a really great relationship. It was theatrical and definitely not your norm. I don't think he ever came outside and played baseball with us. He was very, very feminine.

When it came to Jae's experience with his male peers and whether he experienced bullying growing up, Melissa says,

> *Maybe it's because I was naïve to it, or maybe it really didn't happen. Joe was so kind to everybody. And, you know, he had girlfriends in high school. It wasn't blatant....He had these dramatic, feminine girlfriends for prom, this, that, and the other. But he spent most of his time in the choir and something called Sword and Bauble, which was our drama club. He did a lot of plays, so that was kind of his high school experience. And I really do not remember—even in our neighborhood, where there were boys, and I was always outside playing baseball or whatever they wanted to play, he wouldn't come out, and they didn't ever, that I remember, make any fun of him or bully him or anything. Number one, he was big. But he was so gentle, I just can't even see anybody being mean to him.*

When asked about the Stevens family dynamics, Melissa's tone shifts as she describes a devastating turn of events.

This page: Joseph "Jae" Stevens.
Courtesy of Melissa Honrath.

> *We were good; we were an intact family. But my father was a staunch Republican from Texas....So when my brother was denied the draft because he was gay, my father kicked him out on the spot. So of course, that's when he went to San Francisco. I was a sophomore in high school....That was devastation to our family. He'd already graduated from high school and was going to the junior college, and everything was going along nicely, and then he had to tell my father he was denied from the draft. It broke us—we were all just devastated and wondering, "Where is he going? What's going to happen to him?" We* [kept in contact], *but at the same time, we didn't. We didn't have cell phones; we only had our landline, and we weren't supposed to contact him because of who he was. My mother*

was just crippled by the whole thing. But as it turns out, he went into San Francisco and got into the gay scene, and he started doing a little bit of drag and became very, very popular. Maybe six years later, he was up for a "Golden Globe" in the gay community as the best "female impersonator," and he won that.

The award turned out to be much more than an entertainment accolade. It triggered a monumental change within the family's relationships. Melissa remembers,

Joe was going to the kabuki theater [for the ceremony]—*he actually came back and was living at home—and when he left, he went in drag, and my father bought him a corsage and pinned it on him. I mean, that's the revelation my father must have gone through, to be able to do that. And I'm so proud of my father for that, especially given his background. That was really huge, and it really was a healing moment for our family. So that's pretty much where it was, and then, of course, my mother and I would always go to his shows and see him, and I was always in such awe at how beautiful these men were. God, they were gorgeous. Most of them were lip-syncing.*

"Joe would do Julie Andrews, he did Barbra Streisand, Marilyn Monroe, Petula Clark—that one I don't know why," she laughs.

Melissa loved attending Jae's performances and was elated when she eventually joined him onstage:

Several years into his performances in San Francisco, he decided he wanted to transform into comedy, and so they put together this group, Stevens and Miller and Friends, and it was three gay guys and me. And we performed all over the place. We started out as a cabaret in San Francisco and played there for several months. And of course, everything at that time in your life, when you're in your early twenties, seems like such a long time. I've always been into the performing arts, and I was just kind of hanging out, being a hippie and going back to school, and my brother came and he said, "You know, we really need a girl in this group. And you're talented." And so I joined it, and we were a pretty good hit. So it was Steve Miller, Michael Daily, my brother, and myself. Steve Miller and Joe were the main two characters, Michael Daily and myself sort of filled in for costume changes. It was when Saturday Night Live *first started, that kind of rhythm to*

This page and opposite: Joseph "Jae" Stevens. *Courtesy of Melissa Honrath.*

a performance. We went to Hollywood and all the other clubs coming back up this way [to the Bay Area]. *We were getting ready to go to Boston and the East Coast—which of course, in my mind, if I can get to Boston, I can get to New York, which is really where I wanted to go. Because I* knew *I'd be famous there.*

Melissa laughs, then sighs. "Then that's when Joe was killed. That put an end to the stars in my eyes."

After Jae was found by Spreckels Lake, it was Melissa and her brother William who identified the body. "My parents were both older, anyhow, and they didn't need to do that," Melissa says. If there was a thorough investigation of Jae's murder, Melissa never knew of it. "Nobody, *nobody* did anything about Joe's murder. Nothing. Nothing. My family and myself, we just felt like it was [treated as] 'just another gay bashing' and they don't care."

After Jae's murder, Melissa returned to the police station for the second and final time.

I remember they asked me about his boyfriend, and I cannot remember his name. And they asked me if he had any enemies. I don't remember who I spoke with, but they did ask us some questions. I don't know who it was; it could have been the clerk on duty.

Melissa doesn't remember the name of the man she spoke to or whether he was one of the two homicide detectives originally assigned to the case, Inspectors R. Schneider and A. Podesta. Is it possible either one reached out to anyone else in the family? Melissa says, "I was not living at home, so if they contacted my parents, that's a different situation. I wouldn't know about that, but my parents never said anything to me about it. But I think they would have. We were all pretty devastated."

Melissa later learned of the theory that a serial killer was involved in Jae's murder, and there were potential other victims. Does she think that is what happened?

I don't know. I really don't know....These poor boys. [The police] *weren't caring and trying. My parents weren't notified about even looking for somebody. We were told it was like the 65th homicide or something already that year in this city, my number might be wrong, but* [police were] *just like, "That's too much to deal with." We thought, "Whoa, you guys, this was our brother." It felt like they were treating it like another gay bashing. Like, "Oh well." And we felt helpless; I mean, we didn't know how to do Gay Lives Matter or Black Lives Matter. We were just really good little citizens, being quiet.*

Melissa's memories of Jae and their bond now bring more joy than sadness but still sting at times.

You know, you bury these feelings. But then when I decided to [talk about it], it was really kind of a healing thing....It just felt so unfinished. It's still painful. I just wish my mother and father were still around to really appreciate the efforts that have been going towards Joe.

The pain experienced by the Stevens family neither began nor ended with Jae's death. Jae and Melissa's sister, Teresa, was diagnosed with mental illness in 1972 at the age of sixteen, two years prior to Jae's murder. According to court records, Jae's death triggered a severe psychological break in Teresa; she began to hallucinate figures urging her to kill their mother, Mary. Less than four months after Jae was found dead in Golden Gate Park, Mary's body was recovered from the family home. Teresa had bludgeoned her sleeping mother sometime in the early morning hours. Later that day, Melissa escaped a sledgehammer-wielding Teresa and made it to the Concord police station. Her sister was apprehended and spent the rest of her life in a mental institution. Teresa's psychologists later testified to the link between Jae's murder and that of his mother.

Melissa recalled a journalist who once asked her what she would say to Jae's killer, should he be found. It's a complicated question, and not one with an easy answer. There is one thing she knows she would ask: "Why would you disrupt so many lives? It just wound up creating this ripple effect all the way down to just horrible things."

Chapter 3

THE LAST MEAL

It was late, and thirty-two-year-old Klaus Christmann was hungry. A German immigrant who had worked at a Michelin factory before moving to America, Klaus was married with two children. His family remained overseas but planned to join him stateside soon. In San Francisco, he resided with a man named Booker T. Williams (they met while Williams was in the military and stationed in Germany) and Williams's wife, Nancy. It's unclear as to whether Klaus was closeted, but it is worth noting that while in Germany, he moonlighted at a gay bar. Police would also seize on the fact that he carried with him a tube of makeup on the night he died.

Before Klaus headed back home on the night of July 6, 1974, he stopped at a bar and restaurant named Bojangles, located in the Tenderloin. The prevailing theory later became that while Klaus was enjoying a late-night meal, the killer approached with a finely tuned portrait of brown-haired, gray-eyed Klaus on a napkin or scrap of paper.

At some point, Klaus left Bojangles and was never seen alive again. At 6:29 the following morning, his body was found and reported to police. Tabua Weiss, a Holocaust survivor who, sadly, was no stranger to the wildly horrific, came across him on Ocean Beach while walking her dog. The scene was once again vicious and depraved—but this time, even more so. The coroner summarized:

> *The deceased has four stab wounds in the posterior of his right shoulder, two stab wounds below the right nipple, a large gaping wound of the abdomen and multiple gaping wounds about the neck, in a manner which seemed as*

though the assailant had attempted to decapitate the deceased. There were
no means of identification found on the deceased's person.

When no one came looking for Klaus, the *San Francisco Sentinel* ran a coroner's photo of him and asked the public for help. In the photo, a white sheet is tucked closely underneath Klaus's chin, concealing the gaping wounds that killed him. His eyes and mouth are partially open, a deeply haunting image—one in which it almost appears as though Klaus is taking his last breath.

Twelve days after Klaus's death, Sergeant Elliott Blackstone published his response to a reader's inquiry about the city's gay murder victims in his *San Francisco Sentinel* column, Off the Beat. Blackstone pointed to an unspecified low percentage of overall homicides that involved the gay community and wrote that on the day prior to Jae Stevens's murder, he spoke with the head of the homicide unit regarding that very subject. "I checked and found that we have had a very limited number this year as compared to other years.... As far as I can tell at this point, we've only had six homicides that had gay connotations this year." Klaus's body had yet to be identified, but Blackstone was ready to add his murder to the tally. He wrote that he was "not saying the man [Klaus] was gay—but there were certain factors in terms of physical evidence that give us reason to believe that he may have been."

Unlike Gerald and Jae, Klaus was found with his pants unzipped, though his autopsy does not indicate sexual activity or assault. Underneath his open Levi's jeans, he wore a pair of bright orange shorts, and in his pocket was a tube of makeup. Sergeant Blackstone referenced this evidence in his column: "He may not be gay because clothing can be the same for gay or straight, but he was wearing orange bikini shorts. We're not saying he was definitely gay, but various small factors lead us to that kind of probable belief." That Klaus's body was found on well-known cruising grounds with his pants in the first stages of removal was of no small significance, nor was the fact that Klaus was eventually identified when the autopsy photo was published in a gay newspaper. Whether or not Klaus was indeed closeted is yet to be confirmed; in 2021, Klaus's daughter told Kevin Fagan of the *San Francisco Chronicle* that she wasn't so sure.

Klaus's near-decapitation was not the only element of his murder that stood out from those of Gerald and Jae: he had been not just drunk, but extremely drunk. With a blood alcohol level of 0.33 percent, Klaus was just 0.02 percent away from the lethal tier. Were the violence and the alcohol related? Was the killer just particularly enraged that evening? Did Klaus's inebriation frustrate the killer? One can't be sure—yet.

AT THE TIME OF Klaus's murder, the Zebra killings had plunged San Francisco into chaotic turmoil. The SFPD had received hundreds of tips, one of which would finally pay off and ultimately send Larry Green, J.C.X. Simon, Manuel Moore, and Jessie Lee Cooks to prison for life. But it was another tip, one never connected to the Zebra Murders, that is of interest. One day, around the time of Klaus's murder, someone silently approached a police officer, hands shaking, and gave him a note that read:

ZEBRA
[NAME REDACTED]
POLK ST.
BLACK
MAKEUP
GAY

The person hurried away, refusing to offer a name. What did they know?

Chapter 4

THE TWELFTH APOSTLE

T he level of violence against San Francisco's LGBTQ community in the 1970s was staggering—during the time Gerald, Jae, and Klaus's killer remained free to hunt his victims, police believed there to be at least two other serial killers simultaneously targeting the LGBTQ community in the same area. While the Zebra Murders and the search for the Zodiac Killer dominated headlines, at least seventeen gay men were been murdered, and all signs pointed toward a serial killer or killers perpetrating the crimes.

There were the "Sado Murders" of members of San Francisco's BDSM* community south of Market Street. Late at night, the area commonly known as SoMa was a popular cruising ground for those looking for hookups. It wasn't uncommon for men to openly carry handcuffs, so the presence of restraints would have been no cause for alarm to a potential partner. As a signal, those who wished to dominate wore their keys on their left hip, while those who wished to be dominated wore them on the right.

The alleged murder series began with the brutal slaying of thirty-one-year-old bellhop David Reel (also spelled "Real" in several news articles), who was found by Pacific Gas and Electric workers naked, mutilated, and strangled to death in a parking lot opposite 51 Dore Street on August 29,

---

* BDSM stands for bondage, discipline, dominance, and submission and is a form of consensual sexual activity with participants from a full range of sexual identities. In the 1970s (and in several quotes included in this book), the terms "sado" and "S&M" were used by both critics and participants, referring to sadism and masochism. In modern times, this term can also refer to nonconsensual activity and is not representative of the BDSM community as a whole.

1975. He died before he could arrive at his planned destination, a local gay bar called the Ramrod.

Another victim police publicly linked to the same killer or killers was Dennis Dickinson, whose severely beaten and mutilated body was found inside the fenced schoolyard of the Carmichael School at the corner of Sixth Street and Folsom on July 21, 1975. Dickinson was first thrown into a dumpster, then shortly removed, carried ten feet away, and pummeled even more viciously. Even so, Dickinson survived and dragged himself into a nearby doorway but died before he could be rescued.

Dickinson's death hit the Castro hard. Many loved ones attested to his warm and caring nature, perhaps none better than Damon de Winters, who wrote a short story a month after Dickinson's murder, published in the *Bay Area Reporter*. De Winters describes disciples of Jesus listening to a comforting sermon on acceptance of people some consider to be "different." A dove, representing Dickinson, softly lands on a ledge and listens. De Winters closes the story with,

> *The little dove lifted his slender, silver-grey wings and in leaving sent his shadow rippling over the stained glass. The small group divided itself into individuals and separately each walked up the faded carpet to and through the heavy door. Only sunlight and silence filled the great sleepy yawn again. "How many were there of us?" asked an individual. "Eleven," said a second. "Are you sure?" asked a third? "Yes," said a fourth. "That's strange," mused the fifth, "You're right—but," he paused, "I was almost certain there were twelve."*

Law enforcement appealed to the public for any tips on the cases and were frustrated by the lack of results. As one inspector crudely put it, "Even in the Zebra and mob murders we are getting calls. So far what we've got from the gay community on these murders is almost nothing....It's you people who are dying."

This complete shirking of the police department's responsibility for decades of abuse, harassment, investigative failures, and general acrimony toward the LGBTQ community did not go unnoticed.

Chapter 5

HUNTING THE HUNTER

The San Francisco gay community grew tired of the false promises the SFPD routinely doled out over the years. The streets weren't safer, harassment still happened every day, the nights weren't any less fraught with potential violence. It was time to take matters into their own hands—while remaining within the confines of the law. Multiple organizations were created by citizens for their own protection, with several merging in order to maximize effectiveness.

Bay Area Gay Liberation, or BAGL, turned out at City Hall on February 19, 1975, to protest police harassment and ramp up the pressure on public officials to do something about it. Donald M. Scott, the police chief at the time, had just rolled out an eighteen-point "safer city" program. BAGL argued that several of the plan's points, such as sweeping loitering and curfew laws, directly infringed on the gay community's civil rights. On the day of the protest, over 150 citizens showed up.

BAGL member David C. Goldman described the organization, in an April 1975 letter to the editor of the *Bay Area Reporter*, as one with rotating chairpersons and no official leaders. When it came to the group's goals, strategy, and any other major choices for BAGL, decisions were made democratically—anyone at the meetings participated in the voting process. BAGL was open to the public and welcomed manifold demographics. As Goldman put it, "Our members have varying political philosophies from anarchist to capitalist to communist and socialist….Our diversity gives us strength!"

Gay Action — Responds To Violence

Bay Area Reporter, November 24, 1976.

Despite its intentions, BAGL was covered by the press as a potential cover organization for the communist Social Workers Party. Even the *Bay Area Reporter* suggested this through an unsigned letter to the editor, prompting Goldman's lengthy denunciation of this coverage. "Our group is not a front for the SWP or any other organization. We are a group of people who are dedicated to fighting for gay liberation from a militant, activist perspective." Critics gave BAGL "60 days to 6 months to live." Despite doubt from all sides, BAGL stirred many citizens to action. The openly militant focus of the group stuck as well.

A collective called the Gay Action Community Defense Committee took shape under the umbrella of BAGL. During its first official meeting, attended by over two hundred members, three targeted goals were agreed on: safety, self-defense, and anti-homophobia activism (particularly within the school systems). Many attendees rose to testify of their personal experiences with harassment and assault on the streets of San Francisco, compounded in many cases by police indifference.

The committee voted in support of citizen patrols to protect the gay community from violence and harassment. Patrol members were trained by Ron Lanza, an activist and former schoolteacher. Participants were taught to be on the lookout for potential incidents, as well as how to use restraining force on an attacker until police arrived for an arrest. Lanza was no shrinking violet, either, telling the *San Francisco Examiner*, "This [violence] makes you afraid, but it also makes you strong. Before we were isolated, but now we have a lot of straight support. I know I am not alone." Lanza was also candid on the state of the Castro, saying, "I think we've just seen the tip of the iceberg on what's happening. Many gays are becoming afraid to go out on the streets. But this is our city too, and we're going to take the streets back." Hank Wilson, a teacher in Oakland and member of the Gay Teachers and Schoolworkers' Coalition alongside Lanza, struck a harder tone. In the same *Examiner* piece, Wilson told reporters Ivan Sharpe and Malcolm Glover, "It's just a matter of time before one of those punks gets killed. We're ready for a riot. I'm ready for a riot."

There was good reason to be on edge. "Kevin C." told the *San Francisco Sentinel* of a terrifying incident that occurred on Haight Street in January 1975. Kevin met a man at Gus's, a local bar where he and his friends had been discussing the slew of ongoing murders in the LGBTQ community—several of his chums pointed out to Kevin that he resembled some of the victims. Kevin and the "very pleasant man" left the bar and took a seat at the east entrance of Golden Gate Park. Kevin's new acquaintance was white, about five feet, six inches tall, and weighed 130 to 150 pounds. His blond hair was swept up and back but still hung halfway down his neck.

Without warning, the man drew a weapon. "I saw the knife and didn't believe it," Kevin told the *Sentinel*. "I hesitated. I hesitated too long before I started to run. He stabbed me in the back and in the front again and again. I took my wallet and said, 'Here, take it, I haven't got anything else.' He took it and threw it away and then ran off."

Despite Kevin's knife wounds and the nearby disposal of his wallet, the SFPD assigned a member of the robbery detail, Inspector Joe Goyton, to the case. "There was no robbery involved," Kevin told both the police and the *Sentinel*. "He just pulled out the knife and started stabbing. I figured if I gave him the wallet maybe he would stop." His wounds still healing, Kevin had to pester the SFPD to look at the case. "I had to bug them to even go over mugshots. And Inspector Goyton got upset when I suggested that the case be switched to homicide," Kevin said.

Surviving victims of harassment, assault, and attempted murder were encouraged by the Safe Streets Committee, BAGL, and other associated organizations to provide public testimony and identify their attacker or attackers as best they could. Gay Action member Hal Offen said of the group, "It's difficult for one person to do anything safely, but the patrols make it safer since there will be many of us. I hope that we will inspire other gay people to assist in trouble situations, whether the patrols are there or not." Gay Action's goals were soon shared by another group.

In August 1975, a meeting was called by Mike Rossner to address the rampant violence scattered throughout the Castro. Outrage had finally boiled over after the vicious attack on James Gresham at the Star Pharmacy on Eighteenth and Castro Streets on July 11. Gresham was pushed through a window by four assailants, who later only received misdemeanors—charges that were then dismissed at the arraignment hearing. After public outcry, then–district attorney John J. Ferdon filed new charges of disturbing the peace. The damage had been done.

The new anti-mugging group worked alongside the Safe Streets Committee, which had been formed only a few months prior by attorney

Dick Gayer. He had been fighting for LGBTQ rights for years and was ready to take community action to try to prevent violent attacks. The committee, which in its early stages often consisted of Gayer alone, worked to locate victims and collect their statements. In the process, Gayer would gently nurse their wounds and encourage them to testify against their attackers; some followed through, but many others changed their minds before charges could be filed.

After working tirelessly to build a database of attackers, Gayer steadfastly petitioned law enforcement and the district attorney to file serious charges against perpetrators. Sometimes, this worked. Other times, it did not. There was no shortage of violent incidents—Gayer documented twenty-eight in less than a year, and those were just the ones committed within a two-block radius of Eighteenth and Castro.

With the combined forces of Gayer's and Rossner's citizen support, a plan was laid out to more actively combat violence and harassment. The immediate goal was to provide pocket-size cards with emergency assistance phone numbers to attendees of the 1975 Castro Street Faire, along with educational flyers about the need for more attack prevention. Gayer consistently added new names to his database of criminals, and the group worked to push the courts into action. As Rossner described it, their methods would include "Jewish Defense League tactics"—roving bands of patrollers in the Castro soon took to the streets under his instruction.

Assessment files of SFPD members were created. Policemen who had done their jobs properly and worked hard to protect the gay community were sent letters of commendation. Flyers requested badge numbers and interaction details be sent to the Safe Streets Committee so appreciation could be noted. Reports on law enforcement failures were also mailed to the same address. The names of officers involved in those incidents of misconduct were sent to the SFPD and the district attorney.

Dubbed the "Butterfly Brigade," local citizens patrolled the area armed with radios and whistles to communicate threats and spur immediate action. Incidents ranged from teenagers yelling out slurs from their parents' borrowed cars to attempted beatings, muggings, and worse. Citizen patrols dealt with bigoted youths by recording license plate numbers and notifying the vehicle owners (usually unaware parents) of the incidents. In a show of effort, Captain Rene Aufort of the SFPD's Mission Station assigned one squad car to roam the Castro full time, with additional officers patrolling regularly. Law enforcement frequently crossed paths with the Butterfly Brigade; the patrols wore white headbands, their tall CB radio antennae

The Castro Street Faire, *Bay Area Reporter.*

piercing through the air well above their heads. Glances were exchanged—sometimes with a nod of appreciation, sometimes with a flashed glare.

Plenty of locals also took their safety into their own hands by joining numerous self-defense classes, such as a karate course taught at John Slater's K.E.I. Studio on Polk Street. One student named Dale was a Muni bus driver who had been attacked—and now feared for his life as he watched the murder count in SoMa rapidly rise. After spending seven months training in karate, Dale said of his new strength, "I think it's breaking a pattern of people thinking gays can't defend themselves when [the attackers] are going to come out in worse shape than when they went in."

The Butterfly Brigade, BAGL, Gay Action, Safe Streets Committee, and the LGBTQ community as a whole hoped safety patrols and self-defense training would eventually become unnecessary and the violent atmosphere would cool. As one Butterfly Brigade member, Randy Alfred, put it, "We hope to be so successful that we drive ourselves out of business....I hope we don't have to do this forever." Despite their efforts, at least one serial killer walked the streets freely, perhaps passing by the citizen patrols with a nod and a smile.

Chapter 6

THE WRONG AIR

Yet another string of murders occurred during this time—and in these cases, the target was the transgender community. Barbarella Vasquez was found dead in her apartment at 344 Ellis Street on March 16, 1975, of a single stab wound. The gouge was so deep, police initially thought she had been shot. Just two weeks later, Lisa Rodriguez was found at her home at 370 Ellis Street—less than a block away from the scene of Barbarella's murder. Lisa had also been stabbed; in her case, the knife had struck her five times in the abdomen and back. Three additional victims are known to the public only as Didi, Gina, and Gypsy. The dates, locations, and causes of their deaths have not yet been released.

Barbarella Vasquez was a beloved figure in the trans community of San Francisco in the 1970s, and her death broke many a heart. She was last seen at the Roadrunner, a popular LGBTQ bar, on Friday, March 14, 1975, and left with a friend, Steve Burger, late in the evening. The two relocated to Barbarella's apartment at 344 Ellis Street, where they hung out until the dark of Friday morphed into Saturday's rising sun. Burger told police that Barbarella was still alive at the time of his departure. At ten thirty the following Sunday night, her roommate, known as Gilda Ayala, returned to the apartment to find Barbarella's body, covered in blood, on the sofa. Nothing from the apartment was missing, and the medical examiner noted $105 and jewelry on her person. Whoever killed her hadn't been in it for the money.

Lisa Yancey kept her inner circle small but had a wealth of acquaintances. On the day she died, she spent the morning with Victor, her closest friend.

The two had stayed up through the night with a small band of fellow partiers, and instead of heading to bed, Lisa went straight to Easter services at Glide Methodist Church with her friends Marty, Anne-Marie, and a few others who remain unnamed. Despite the lack of sleep, Lisa, as always, was dressed to the nines for the ceremony. She stepped out of the house in black patent leather loafers with gold trim, crisp white pants with brown stitching and trim, a gold and brown T-shirt, and a tan waist-length jacket topped with a fabulous fur collar. Her hair was perfect. Marty later described Lisa as incredibly generous and almost whimsically spontaneous—sometimes she'd drop everything to take a friend to Tijuana just for breakfast.

Following Easter services, the group began to disperse, as several of its members were finally in dire need of some sleep. Lisa, on the other hand, held a standing reservation at the *PS Lounge at 1121 Polk Street for Saturday brunch and was ready for a meal. They all strolled to Union Square, about six blocks from the restaurant, to sort out a plan. Victor decided to head home but saw Lisa hours later, still at Union Square, soaking in the sunshine. The upper class was parading its Easter fashion around the block, and Lisa had stayed to enjoy the view. When it came to potential love interests, she had zero tolerance for sloppy dress or anything other than a manicured appearance. A man needed to be "masculine" but not "macho"; presenting too "feminine" an appearance was also a deal-breaker, a friend told the press.

After Lisa had her fill of people-watching, she and Victor decided to finally get that brunch at *PS. Following the meal, a potential trip to the movies was tossed about, but the two separated again, as Victor hadn't gotten the sleep he so desperately wanted. It was the last time he saw Lisa alive.

Anne-Marie's birthday was coming up, and Lisa was planning a surprise party for her on the upcoming Wednesday, four days after Victor and Lisa's brunch. Ginnie, a mutual friend of the group, called Lisa on Monday to check in on the status of the party preparations. The phone continuously rang with no answer. Assuming Lisa was simply out of the apartment, she decided to try again the next day. When she had no better luck on Tuesday, she called Marty (a fellow Easter Sunday comrade), hoping for an update. That night, Marty headed to Lisa's apartment with a key she had given him. The moment he opened the door, he knew something was terribly amiss.

As Marty put it, the air was wrong. The apartment was always in impeccable order—but after walking through the hallway, Marty entered the living room to find the pictures Lisa so lovingly hung on the walls had been viciously torn down. Bed covers and pillows were strewn about on the floor. Marty's thoughts went straight to burglary, so he immediately began the arduous task of piecing the apartment together. After pulling back one of the sheets bunched up on the floor, Marty found Lisa and rushed to telephone the police. She had been stabbed three times in the back and twice in the abdomen. One hand tightly clasped strands of long, dark hair. On the floor lay a roll of exposed film—police later believed it was torn from a camera because it contained a photograph of Lisa's killer. Two sets of unidentified fingerprints were lifted from inside the apartment.

When the *San Francisco Sentinel* covered the crimes on April 10, 1975, reporter Dave Johns wrote,

> *People in the area talk of a sick killer walking unknown into the bars and coolly picking his victims. Inspector Manley of Homicide said that the recent murders of [Lisa] and Barbarella as well as others in the past year have been thoroughly compared by the crime lab and do not appear to be the work of the same person.*

The theory was based on hair samples taken from both scenes that didn't match each other (it's notable that hair analyses lacking DNA comparison have been overwhelmingly discredited since 1975). Also, Barbarella was killed with one stroke versus the five stab wounds Lisa received, and law enforcement had no witnesses linking the two.

The police's theory that the murders were unrelated just didn't hold water to many in the gay community. Barbarella's and Lisa's murders were not investigated by Gilford and Sanders but rather two separate investigators altogether. Inspector Manley was assigned to Lisa's case, while Inspector Nelson headed up the search for Barbarella's killer. These details did the opposite of bolster the LGBTQ community's faith in the SFPD.

In April 1975, fifty-six citizens gathered at the Helping Hands Center in San Francisco for a meeting on Barbarella and Lisa's murders. One person helping lead the discussion was Marty, the man who found Lisa's body.

Helping Hands existed alongside several other organizations dedicated to serving San Francisco's transgender community. The group provided a wide range of services, including locating transgender-safe rental units, recommending doctors who were educated on and supportive of transgender medical needs, and advising on how to apply makeup.

At the Helping Hands meeting for Barbarella and Lisa, many demands for justice were made. Popular Tenderloin performer Miss Carol Lynn called for those present to work together and create a network of contacts to gather information that would lead to the killer or killers' arrest. Flyers advertising a $500 reward offered by the Tavern Guild, a collective that represented over one hundred gay bars and restaurants, went up across the Castro and Tenderloin districts. Law enforcement noticed.

When Helping Hands gathered for a second meeting, Inspector Hobart Nelson of the homicide unit showed up. Nelson promised to investigate the case until it was solved, as well as treat the murder of a member of the LGTBQ community just as he would any other. Nelson told the crowd, "Despite what you have heard, I myself consider gay people, transsexuals, all people, first-class citizens, and I work just as hard on a killing of one of your people as I do on the murder of a wealthy person." He made it clear, however, that he was only speaking for himself.

Chapter 7

THE FINAL BATTLE

Frederick Elmer Capin was an artist, just as legend would have his killer. The press called his paintings "promising," but his most notable accomplishments occurred while serving his country and serving it well. His abilities as a Navy medical corpsman were of the highest caliber—even under fire. After a turbulent and sometimes brutal childhood, he had entered into service on a path to a brighter future. The military provided an escape from oft-inebriated parents and unpredictable stints in foster homes. Fred rescued four Marines from enemy attack in Vietnam and earned the Navy and Marine Corps Commendation Medal for valor. Despite the weight of his achievements, Fred was only thirty-two and preparing to begin a new chapter of his life.

Following a distinguished career in the Navy, Fred found himself in San Francisco. But the city that had so closely drawn him in was starting to wear on him. The bright lights of the Castro began to dim under the dark cloud of muggings and murders that seeped through the streets. Fred told his family to skip the visit they had been planning; he was ready to move on and resettle in Washington State. After all, it was where he had shared his grandparents' home while furthering his education. It was where his beloved sister, Gretchen, still lived.

Fred was younger than he looked; the coroner later described him as "a well-developed, wiry, well-muscled young white man who appears to be 20–25 years of age." Fred was a lean six feet tall and 148 pounds, and his hazel eyes rested between brunette hair and a red-tinged mustache he had just begun to grow.

Fred wasn't a wallflower by appearance. On the night of May 11, 1975, he selected a Picasso shirt, a blue corduroy jacket, jeans overtop blue shorts, and a brown woven belt with a yellow buckle. This was what he was found wearing when Christopher Griffin discovered him the next morning on the same blood-soaked stretch of Ocean Beach as Gerald and Klaus. For detectives, the case's eerie similarities to the others were immediately apparent.

Fred was sprawled approximately forty feet west of Great Highway, near Pacheco Street. His jacket and shirt were bunched under his head and covered with blood, with smears on the soles of both shoes and his hands, face, and upper torso on all sides. Twenty-foot drag marks in the sand leading to his body indicated a potential struggle and an attempt to move Fred away from the popular walking path where he was killed.

The knife struck Fred sixteen times, nicking his sternum and a rib in the process. Gashes above his right hand and forearm indicated to the coroner that Fred attempted a lightspeed defense but to no avail. The majority of the stabs were found around Fred's heart—along with a cluster that crossed his chest and connected his nipples. His right lung had collapsed. Still, Fred had not gone down without a fight; all of his wounds were on the front of his body. At some point, either Fred or his killer had unbuttoned his pants, but his autopsy showed no physical signs of sexual activity.

Like Gerald, Fred hadn't had a drop to drink that night, but even without impairing substances, he was overpowered by the killer. Had the two crossed paths along Ocean Beach? After the SFPD interviewed several witnesses, Fred was placed at Bojangles, where he had a bite to eat—just as Klaus did prior to his murder. It all added up.

Fred was stripped of his identification, but the fingerprints included in his military records provided Gilford and Sanders with his name and personal details. That he saved the lives of four countrymen in Vietnam and finally returned stateside only to be murdered in cold blood on a dark night in a city he'd grown tired of is particularly painful to loved ones. His body rests where he intended to thrive: a plot in Bremerton, Washington.

Chapter 8

THE MAN IN BLUE

Harald Gullberg was different from the other Doodler victims. Born in Sweden in 1908, Harald was sixty-six years old when his life was taken by the killer—significantly older than Gerald, Jae, Klaus, or Frederick. A second, much grimmer aspect of his murder would also stand out: unlike the other victims, who were found shortly after they were killed, Harald lay hidden in the brush at Lands End for at least ten days. Found horribly decomposed by a passerby on June 4, 1975, Harald had been stabbed, with slashes to his aorta ending his life. A second factor also stood out from the other victims: police believed that Harald's underwear had been removed and taken from the scene. Did Klaus's and Fred's unbuttoned pants indicate their killer had tried and failed to do this to them as well?

Lands End is a renowned hiking location, secluded from many a passerby. Dramatic cliffs drop down into the churning Pacific, with the park's trail ending at Sutro Baths, a gigantic saltwater swimming pool that burned down to its foundation in June 1966. The remaining concrete blocks that sit at the water's edge create platforms from which tourists and residents alike take in the stunning vista, many unaware of the spot's past inferno. Thick groves of trees alongside dense brush create natural enclosures seemingly perfect for a discreet rendezvous with a postcard backdrop. It was here that Harald was led into the dark and left to bleed out, a mere ten yards away from the trail.

Until 2021, very little was known about Harald, originally identified as John Doe #81. When a team of freelance correspondents in Sweden was hired by reporter Kevin Fagan of the *San Francisco Chronicle* in 2020 for his investigation of the Doodler Murders, a fuller picture of Harald's life emerged. As a sixteen-year-old merchant sailor, Harald lied about his age as a way to leave his hometown of Ekeby and travel the world. An unidentified surviving niece told Fagan she often wondered whether Harald's sexuality was a factor in his departure from everything he knew. Tragically, the sea—his mode of escape into a new life—would set the scene for his violent death.

We know Harald loved the color blue—so much so, in fact, that on the night of his murder he donned blue socks, blue pants, a blue shirt, and a blue windbreaker. Before the stabbing began, the windbreaker was removed—following the murder, it was replaced and zipped to the neck. Blood covered Harald's blue shirt from his neck to his waist; a grisly scene, but so were all the others. Why were his wounds covered? What did that mean to investigators?

Harald's murder was assigned to Detectives Gilford and Sanders. While Bennett Cohen, who coauthored Sanders's book on the Zebra Murders, remembers discussing the Doodler killings with Sanders, details such as the windbreaker and whether the implications of its placement were explored are sealed along with the rest of the case file, if they exist at all. Sanders and Gilford were known for tireless dedication to their caseload and had been building a profile of Harald's killer, so it's likely those notes were taken—and, hopefully, preserved.

Harald's teeth, on the other hand, were not. His degenerated dental state was severe enough for current independent investigators to theorize he had been homeless. In reality, when police searched Harald's room at a local mariners' boardinghouse, they found a sizeable heap of cash tucked away. He frequently moved; it made sense to avoid the complications of multiple banks.

Harald's murder did not mark a dead end of clues. The most shocking details about the killer, his methods, and his motive were yet to come. Up until their deaths, the killer's victims were the silenced witnesses to his atrocities. But the public would soon learn they were not alone—three survivors had a story to tell.

Chapter 9

ALL THE SAME

About a month after Harald's body was found, in July 1975, the killer sought out his next victim. This time, the pickup happened at the Truck Stop, a late-night diner on Market Street. The time was approximately two o'clock in the morning.

The victim was a man later known only as "the Diplomat," a reference to his career. While it's unclear which exact position he held (that detail is reserved for the SFPD case file), his Scandinavian accent provides a clue to independent investigators. Perhaps it's a coincidence the Diplomat shared that attribute with Harald. Perhaps not.

The killer approached his victim with drawings of animals—this later spawned sprawling theories as to the Doodler's method of murder, promoted by both the press as well as Gilford and Sanders. In the case of the Diplomat, it is true his attacker displayed a skilled hand and spoke of being a commercial art student.

The two departed the Truck Stop and headed to the victim's apartment in the Fox Plaza at 1390 Market Street, a few blocks away. The next time the Diplomat exited his front door, he was forever changed.

The attack was swift and rage-fueled, just as the others had been. But this time, detectives obtained details on the killer's motivation. Prior to the attempted murder, the Doodler had requested cocaine. This is the first mention of any drugs linked to the killer—none of his victims tested positive for any over-the-counter, prescribed, or illicit substances.

The killer entered the Diplomat's bathroom, where he would stay for thirty minutes before he emerged and told the victim, "You people are all the same." He spewed his anger at the Diplomat, saying, "I've done this before and I enjoy this. Your anguish and pain and everything else [are] something I enjoy." The Diplomat was clear on the intent— "you people" meant gay men. Some version of this hateful statement was later said to other survivors as well.

The knife struck the Diplomat with blinding force—the blows so powerful, the blade finally broke from the handle. The victim took the opportunity to shove the Doodler into a wall—enough of a threat that he immediately fled. Yet the attacker got more daring after that narrow escape, crafting his techniques to achieve bolder kills. His next attempt was jaw-dropping in its audacity.

A week and a half after the Diplomat escaped certain death, his attempted killer returned to the Fox Plaza. Not only did the man return to the building, but he also revisited the same floor, choosing a "local public figure" who lived practically next door to the Diplomat. This time, the Doodler upped the odds in his favor—this is the first attack known to the public where the killer employed some form of restraints on his victim. It's unclear whether tying up his prey was part of consensual foreplay or forced on the victim. The press reported that when the survivor screamed so loudly that his neighbors began to pound on the walls, his attacker was forced to once again flee the Fox Plaza.

Unsatisfied, the Doodler sought out a high-profile victim next. Described by Gilford and Sanders as a renowned figure and household name, the target was a Los Angeles–based entertainer who was visiting San Francisco. This time, the victim escaped unscathed—physically, at least. The two were starting to get into bed when a knife fell out of the killer's pocket, and the victim's quick thinking to immediately run out the door saved his life. The attack was within days of the Doodler's second Fox Plaza victim.

With three surviving witnesses, the case appeared to be nearing a close. But it would be society—not the killer—that would guard their silence. For the victims to publicly disclose their trauma would only immeasurably amplify it; it would mean breaking up their families, destroying their careers, annihilating the things they held most dear. The Doodler had stolen enough

Survivors Won't Talk— Gay Killing Case Stalls

San Francisco Sentinel.

from them. He would not take any more. As of 2022, the identities of all three survivors remain sealed in the SFPD's case files.

While the lack of public testimony stalled out the investigation, the victims simultaneously provided the biggest break in the case. A picture emerged: a drawing of the killer not unlike those police said he drew to lure in his victims. When the SFPD held a press conference in October 1975 and released a composite sketch, it was a face that some in the public soon recognized.

Chapter 10

TO SPITE HIS FACE

The 1975 image that surfaced from the memories of the surviving victims of the Doodler was one of a young man who should have been in the prime of his life; a man just entering the fullness of adulthood, one who instead of building his own future was obliterating at least five others'; a cold-blooded killer whose list of victims within just two years is longer than that of other twisted "careers" spanning decades. His number of alleged murders matches the Zodiac and Jack the Ripper. Ted Kaczynski, also known as the Unabomber, murdered three victims. David Berkowitz, whose moniker Son of Sam was splashed across hundreds of headlines, exceeded the Doodler's body count by just one—according to the SFPD tally in 1976. Yet the police sketch barely circulated within San Francisco, let alone across the country.

The killer, aged nineteen to twenty-one, was a lanky, six-foot-tall Black male sporting a Navy watch cap. His eyes peered out from below a pronounced brow ridge, resting above a slightly downturned mouth. He had told both the Diplomat and other survivors that he was a commercial art student. Based on the survivors' reports, Gilford began to build a profile of the Doodler. He told the *San Francisco Chronicle* he thought the killer likely had a "quiet, serious personality, probably with an upper middle-class education and above-average intelligence. But he's having difficulty with his sexuality. He's probably ashamed of what he's doing....The guilt he is experiencing causes him to want to erase the acts he's committed." Charles Lee, a *San Francisco Sentinel* writer, told the *Chronicle* he believed "the Doodler is attracted and

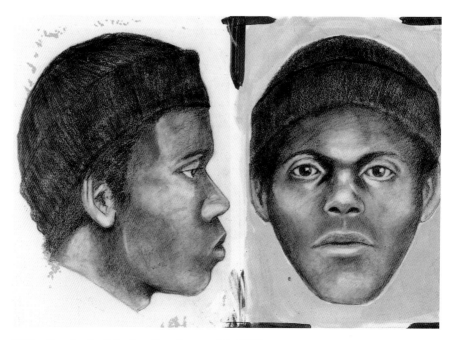

1975 police sketch of the Doodler. *Courtesy of the SPFD.*

repelled by gays. This sets up a guilt syndrome. The only way he can assuage his guilt is by killing. That proves to him he's not really a homosexual." Lee also theorized the Doodler posed as a sex worker to pick up his victims.

A steady stream of tips began to flow to Detectives Gilford and Sanders. After a receptionist at a local psychiatrist's office saw the composite sketch, both she and her employer recognized the face as one of their patients. The psychiatrist, noted in records with the potential last name "Priest," provided his October 1975 report to police after three prior attempts made by at least one woman who worked in his Highland Hospital office in Oakland. The initial outreach included a name, the second a license plate, the third details on the alleged killer's psychiatric treatment, and the fourth finally came in from the psychiatrist himself. He was confident the patient should be considered in the Doodler case, and he wanted the SFPD to know. At last, Gilford and Sanders felt they were on their way to nabbing a suspect.

The patient was identified and hauled into police headquarters. He described how he had cured his past gay "tendencies" and said he was living in the East Bay with a girlfriend. The methods employed by "Dr. Priest" during the patient's "curing" process are unknown; the possibilities range from pseudoscientific "therapy" to chemical castration.

Lieutenant Charles Ellis briefs the press on the Doodler murders in 1975. *Courtesy of the SPFD.*

The patient's openness with Gilford and Sanders wasn't hard-won; the detectives described him as willingly helpful—but his steadfast denial of the murders put an end to the interrogation. Yet when this man was brought into SFPD headquarters for an eight-man lineup, the Diplomat recognized his face but would not go on the record in order to help police make an arrest. Without public testimony or physical evidence, the congenial suspect was free to leave.

The patient of Dr. Priest was not the only person of interest police wanted to question. A few months after the SFPD was contacted by the psychiatrist's office, a tip came in about a man who fit the description and was outside of a Tenderloin bar, peddling drawings. Police headed over and picked him up. He did indeed match the composite sketch. He was at a gay bar, offering to draw patrons. And when he was approached by law enforcement, a butcher knife slid out of his sleeve, clanking against the pavement. He was put in handcuffs and taken to the station. When he arrived, he put up a fight. On top of a concealed weapon charge, the suspect landed himself a count of aggravated assault when he attacked unnamed investigators during the interrogation. Was he the Doodler?

Chapter 11

BAD MEDICINE

Two years before the Doodler's first murder, the American Psychiatric Association held its annual meeting in 1972 at Temple University in Philadelphia. The attendants knew the panel assembled onstage would be lively. The topic at hand was whether homosexuality, which had been classified as a mental disorder up until that point, should remain as such. There had been multiple protests leading up to the meeting, and the panel members knew the outrage could no longer be ignored. The *Diagnostic and Statistical Manual of Mental Disorders* (commonly referred to as the *DSM*) was in its second edition, and a growing number of both psychiatrists and patients called for the "diagnosis" of homosexuality as a mental illness to be removed from its pages.

A man dressed in a suit and oversize bowtie took the microphone. He wore a warped rubber Richard Nixon mask, commonly sold in costume shops at the time. Before he spoke into the microphone, he employed a voice distortion box to further hide his identity.

The man, who called himself Dr. H. Anonymous, began his speech with the words, "I am a homosexual. I am a psychiatrist. I, like most of you in this room, am a member of the APA and am proud of that membership." The panel members were selected to discuss the designation of homosexuality as a mental disorder, but the group of speakers was composed of APA members who were *either* gay *or* a psychiatrist. Here, Dr. Anonymous would provide valuable insight and serve as the only contributor to the conference

Right: Dr. John Fryer
speaking as Dr. Henry
Anonymous. *Photo by
Kay Tobin. Courtesy of the
Equality Forum.*

Below: APA protesters
outside of the Supreme
Court. *Photo by Harry
Goodman. Courtesy of the D.C.
Public Library.*

who would speak from this perspective. Other gay psychiatrists were,
validly, hesitant to touch the subject for fear of losing their jobs (such as
Dr. John E. Fryer, who had been fired from his residency at the University
of Pennsylvania after being told, "If you were gay and not flamboyant, we
would keep you. If you were flamboyant and not gay, we would keep you.
But since you are both gay and flamboyant, we cannot keep you").

Dr. Anonymous continued to speak, encouraging fellow psychiatrists
to simply listen to what he had to say, rather than attempt to discern his
identity. He referred to the "Gay PA" in acknowledgement of his fellow gay

psychiatrists in attendance, many of whom were still closeted. He ended with a direct plea to those who wanted to remain so:

> *For all of us have something to lose. We may not be considered for that professorship, the analyst down the street may stop referring us his overflow, our supervisor may ask us to take a leave of absence. We are taking an even bigger risk, however, in not living fully our humanity, with all of the lessons it has to teach all the other humans around us.*

At first glance, it would seem Dr. Anonymous (through his name, costume, and change of voice) was trying to remain closeted. However, that was far from the case. Dr. Anonymous wanted his speech to represent more than just him individually; he wanted to call attention to the significant number of psychiatrists who themselves were gay, and that group needed to be acknowledged. After a subsequent interview during a two-hour broadcast of a local radio show, Dr. Anonymous remained so until the 1994 APA convention in Philadelphia, where he officially revealed himself to be Dr. John E. Fryer.

IN 1973, HOMOSEXUALITY WAS removed as a mental disorder in the *DSM-III*. While the change was far from perfect (it still noted that the absence of heterosexual desire *may* indicate psychopathology), this step toward justice and humanity was hard-won and saved numerous gay patients from becoming institutionalized or forced participants in what was then called "conversion therapy." This form of psychological (and sometimes physical) abuse ranged from hours of repetitive "therapy" sessions to barbaric attempts to change the gay "condition," including electroshock therapy and chemical castration. In a 1991 study conducted by Dr. Doug Haldeman, long-term effects of "conversion therapy" (now referred to as conversion efforts, so as to not legitimize a practice that serves as the antithesis of proper therapy) included depression, a sense of failure, and suicidal thoughts.

In 1973, the year before the Doodler Murders began, the California Council on Criminal Justice approved a violence control program at the University of California, Los Angeles. The program would allow police and prison officials to employ a wide range of extreme punishments—including chemical castration of those considered to be "sexual deviants." Legislators denied the program funding—but not indefinitely. Many didn't outright oppose the program; they just wanted more details.

The Committee Opposing Abuse of Psychiatry met on January 19, 1974, at the First Unitarian Church in San Francisco to organize against the "violence prevention" program. A spokesperson for the committee told the *San Francisco Sentinel* of how the program could turn California "into a therapeutic police state like 'A Clockwork Orange.'...In this police state, doctors would replace the cops on the beat, deciding who is likely to become violent and putting this person into what amounts to preventative detention." The committee knew the pressure needed to be back on lawmakers to continue the refusal to fund the program. As the *Sentinel* put it, "Californians are confronted with the very real danger of a therapeutic police state in which preventative detention will be justified as therapy," in addition to a concentration on "individuals pseudo-scientifically pronounced as a 'violent-prone' culture." In other words, the gay community would have a target on its back.

The fear was validated by the United States government itself. The program was proposed under newly appointed attorney general Elliot Richardson. Richardson was promoted from the secretary of health, education and welfare, where he was known as the "secretary of lobotomy." Prior to being promoted to attorney general, Elliot created a pilot program for the use of lobotomies to "cure" non-heterosexual desires; three were performed by Dr. Walter Freeman at the Atascadero State Hospital and three by an undisclosed doctor at Vacaville Prison. An untold number of procedures were performed on inmates at other federal and state prisons.

Elliot became attorney general under President Richard Nixon. The two had worked together for years and secured funding for a lobotomy center facilitated by the Federal Bureau of Prisons in 1971. Elliot and Nixon's approval of lobotomies used on LGBTQ citizens as a "cure" was not supported by the data. Since the procedure consisted of removing the part of the brain that processes sexual desire, postoperative patients did not awake heterosexual but rather without any sexual desire whatsoever. The surgery had not "converted" the patients; rather, it served to destroy part of the essence of their natural being. The evidence made no difference in Elliot and Nixon's minds; to them, the result was all the same.

The UCLA violence prevention program staff wasn't formed yet, but one top selection horrified the gay community. Dr. Hunter Brown had performed numerous lobotomies on gay inmates in California prisons for years—it was one of his proudest accomplishments. His career was focused on the practice to such a degree that there was a period of time during which he provided the State of California with free services in exchange for permission to perform experimental brain surgeries on "habitually criminal" inmates. Alongside Brown, Dr. Frank Ervin was also a top contender to lead the program; he supported lobotomizing gay citizens so steadfastly that he wrote a book on it—subsidized by the Nixon administration.

Less than three months after the Committee Opposing Abuse of Psychiatry met in San Francisco to protest Elliot and Nixon's proposed violence prevention center at UCLA, the House Judiciary Committee started impeachment proceedings against Nixon. Lobotomies and gay "conversion" were now the last thing on his mind.

DESPITE THE DECLASSIFICATION OF homosexuality as a mental illness in 1973, conversion efforts live on to this day. Under the cloak of claimed religion, a number of organizations continue to advertise themselves as a "cure" for anything outside of a heterosexual identity. As these groups work outside of the regulated world of psychiatry, they are protected by U.S. law in a multitude of ways that certified practitioners are not.

Back in the 1970s, the harmful impact of conversion efforts was widely unknown to the public, and the practice existed much as it had prior to the updated *DSM-III*. Its status diminished over time, however, since it had been discarded by the American Psychiatric Association. In an effort to conjure faux credibility, the National Association for Research and Therapy of Homosexuality (also called NARTH) was formed in the 1990s. This pseudoscience organization was soon embraced by anti-LGBTQ groups, which sunk millions into this attempt to legitimize "therapy" that had, at that point, been widely documented as harmful to participants. Because NARTH was steeped in dogmatic religion, the burden of pursuing any form of accountability fell to activists rather than Congress. These advocates for justice continue their work to this day through organizations such as the United States Joint Statement, which partners with major medical and psychological associations to raise awareness of the dangers of conversion efforts.

The hard-fought battle of Dr. Fryer, known as Dr. Anonymous for decades, had been won to a degree in the 1970s, but organizations such as NARTH were able to continue their abusive practices unscathed. It's very likely that few to none of their "patients" were aware of the updates to the *DSM-III*. What's more, would it really matter? Society had already decided what the LGBTQ community represented, and the *DSM* made little difference to many. Some conversion efforts centers continue to thrive to this today.

Chapter 12

INSULT TO INJURY

While all indications point to Detectives Gilford and Sanders actively investigating the murders, the gravity of the killings was not appreciated by all members of the SFPD. "We feel they are emotionally unstable," said Captain William O'Connor, head of the SFPD's public relations unit, of the gay community in 1975. When challenged by the public, O'Connor referred to the deep-seated aversion of the SPFD to the gay community: "I just recalled what standard police training manuals say about homosexuals."

O'Connor, like the majority of San Francisco, was unaware of the American Psychiatric Association's removal of homosexuality as a mental disorder from its textbooks two years prior. When asked whether he was aware of gay members of the SFPD, he responded with, "No! But I'd sure like to have a list of them." Chairman of the Pride Foundation Paul Hardman campaigned for O'Connor's resignation, saying,

> This attitude may be why the San Francisco Police Department finds itself incapable of solving crimes where gay people are the victims.... His comments are improper in the legal sense of that word. We have ordinances against this kind of attitudinal direction. Perhaps it's time we had a complete change of higher posts within the police department. We need younger officers who are more in touch with the community at large in the department.

With police protection a rarity for most members of the gay community, many walked the city at night with valid uncertainty they could make it home safely. The Safe Streets Committee, BAGL, Gay Action, and others were hard at work providing as much protection as possible against an onslaught of assaults, murders, muggings, kidnappings, and more. A hotline was established for citizens to report incidents and ask for help.

In particular, a wave of violent muggings gripped the headlines of San Francisco's gay publications, and it turned out Lands End and Ocean Beach were the hunting grounds for more than just the Doodler. On August 10, 1975, five teenage boys roamed Lands End wielding swords and knives, searching specifically for gay men. The group proclaimed themselves to be "roisting the f—ts," so much so that when they accidentally robbed a straight victim, they returned the twenty dollars he gave them and moved on in search of a correctly acquired target. The victim found a squad car nearby; while he was reporting the incident, another officer came over the radio to request assistance with a robbery. The five boys were arrested at a bus stop; they had tossed their weapons into a bush close to the scene. After one gang member was taken to the juvenile division of the SFPD, his parents declined to pick him up at the station until the following morning, as they felt he should be punished for his crimes. It is quite possible this was the harshest repercussion he faced for committing a felony.

Chapter 13

DEEP TROUBLES

During the original investigation, police maintained the Doodler killed between five and fourteen victims (though some reports note a possible total of sixteen). Who were these other potential victims of the Doodler? Why are their identities only tentatively mentioned? One might think building a list of homicides that fit the Doodler case's known elements (white, male, gay victims who were stabbed in San Francisco from 1974 to 1975) would yield a manageable pool of potentially linked victims. The reality is much darker.

Gerald, Jae, Klaus, Frederick, and Harald all were killed and left outdoors. Known survivors of the Doodler, however, were nearly killed in their own apartments. This changes everything, as a change in the location of the attempted murders indicates that the killer was evolving his methods. The Doodler felt comfortable entering victims' homes, their safest spaces, and destroying all in his wake. To uncover his other potential murders means widening the search to include homicides that occurred in the victim's home. Two of the Doodler survivors were attacked in the same apartment building, the Fox Plaza. Was there a third neighbor who didn't survive?

THE FOX PLAZA GREW into a fabled destination of death to those familiar with its history. To many, this high-rise apartment building is simply a long-standing piece of San Francisco's skyline, but to a significant number of residents, it became the scene of their deaths—many by suicide.

Fox Plaza. *Photo by Terri Meyer Boake. Courtesy of the artist.*

'Senseless murder':

ANOTHER STABBING --AT FOX PLAZA SEPT. 28

George J. Gilbert, 32, was found stabbed to death in his Fox Plaza apartment Monday, September 29. He became a cause of concern when he failed to appear at work that morning, and a longtime friend gained entry to Gilbert's apartment and found the nude body in bed.

Top: Still from the 1973 film *The Laughing Policeman. 20th Century Studios.*

Bottom: San Francisco Sentinel.

Myth has it the Fox Plaza, built in 1966, was cursed by Anton LaVey, the founder of the Church of Satan, as it replaced his beloved Fox Theatre. LaVey claimed to have performed on the organ at the theater eleven days prior to the first strike of the wrecking ball; this, however, has yet to be confirmed. One moment in the history of the Fox Plaza is certain, though— the murder of George Gilbert.

On September 29, 1975, a few months after the Doodler's attempts on two lives at the Fox Plaza, thirty-two-year-old resident George Gilbert was found dead in his apartment. An assistant trust officer at a nearby Wells Fargo bank, Gilbert had gone home for the night after enjoying his evening watching a film at the Ramrod, where David Reel, the bellhop who was found by Pacific Gas and Electric workers strangled in a parking lot, was also last seen. Gilbert led a closeted life and felt free to express himself in such establishments; their proximity to his home allowed him to patronize these bars frequently.

Friends later revealed Gilbert's sexuality, which the press seized on, dubbing him a "leather freak, 'slave' who liked being gagged, tied down on all fours, and spanked to the point of orgasm." Newspapers justified these sensationalist quotes since Gilbert, found without any notable defense wounds, was likely tied up consensually prior to his death. Media reports assumed sexual activity occurred between the killer and his victim. Gilbert's autopsy revealed the contrary.

Gilbert's blood alcohol level was 0.19 percent when he was stabbed eight times in his lower abdomen. Regarding any other substances (including over-the-counter medications), none were present, just as the Doodler victims' autopsies had noted. Samples taken from both the mouth and rectum showed no presence of sexual activity or assault. No foreign objects were found in the bladder or rectum. But the killer did leave something behind apart from stab wounds so deep Gilbert's body was found with his intestines partially protruding. Included in his autopsy is a note on "a series of four symmetrical areas...suggestive of bite marks."

A COMPARISON OF GILBERT'S murder and the Doodler's known victims shows several key differences. However, this certainly doesn't rule out the possibility that Gilbert's murder was committed by the same man who killed Gerald, Jae, Klaus, Frederick, and Harald. A comparison between Gilbert and one survivor highlights this potential.

Gilbert was tied up—just as the second Fox Plaza survivor had been. The Fox Plaza survivor's screams alerted neighbors and forced the killer to flee. Is it possible that the last face Gilbert saw was the same menacing visage seen by the Ocean Beach, Golden Gate Park, and Lands End victims?

To many, the bite marks on Gilbert could be seen as a key part of forensic evidence. Thorough studies conducted within the past decade, however, paint a different picture. The National Academies Review found little scientific support for bitemark analysis, and even worse, a significant number of convictions based on bitemark analysis have been overturned after DNA exoneration.

Prior to 1974, the work of forensic dentists was almost entirely focused on identifying bodies by comparative analysis using dental records and other means. A sudden shift occurred that year, and ever since then, much of the general public has been under the impression that bitemarks are nearly as reliable a form of evidence as fingerprints.

Forensic dentistry is not the only subsection of forensic science that has been challenged. In 1979, voiceprint analysis was disproven and subsequently abandoned by courts after data showed the field's gaping inaccuracies. This is applicable to the known evidence in the case of Gerald's 1974 murder—the recording of a 911 call reporting the body. It, like the bitemarks on Gilbert, is, unfortunately, not as significant a clue as one might assume. It would take much more to connect, let alone solve, both Gilbert's and Gerald's murders.

A MONTH AFTER THE attack on Gilbert, the Doodler composite sketch was released to the public. Dianne Feinstein, a member of San Francisco's board of supervisors at the time, had set her eyes on the mayorship. Before her campaign closed with a loss by 1 percent of the vote, she focused heavily on San Francisco's gay community and spoke of the widespread hunting of its members in a statement:

> *I am deeply troubled by the more than twelve brutal gay murders which have taken place in San Francisco recently. Many of these murders appear to be related and suggest that a sadistic murderer or murderers are at large.*
>
> *Recently the first considerable body of information about these murders was given to me by members of the gay community. I said then publicly, and I repeat it now, we cannot tolerate the lack of a major investigation into these horrible crimes. When I am elected Mayor, I will insist upon a strong and vigorous investigation into these and all murders that take place in San Francisco.*

AT CANDIDATES' NIGHT:

FEINSTEIN BLASTS P.D. FOR UNSOLVED CASES

Left: San Francisco Sentinel, October 9, 1975.

Below: Dianne Feinstein speaking with reporters. *Photo by Bernard Gotfryd. Courtesy of Library of Congress.*

> *Until then I will continue to relay information given to me to the homicide bureau and will remain in close contact with the police department.*
>
> *In short, under my administration there will be commissions and departments responsive to and representative of ALL people. And the gay community, rather than being set apart, will be a part of an active and involved citizenry having its voice heard in the Mayor's office at City Hall.*

While Feinstein did not eke out an election win and make it to city hall that year, a major political figure had, at length, acknowledged the magnitude of the murders and the lack of progress in the investigation. It was not enough in the end.

WHEN A SPECIAL INVESTIGATION Squad was formed by the SFPD the following year to specifically target murderers stalking the gay community, two detectives were glaringly absent. Gilford and Sanders, who had by then put over a year of work into searching for the Doodler, weren't invited. Out of the entire homicide unit, by many accounts, they were the most trusted detectives within the gay community. Chief of Inspectors Mortimer McInerney told the press of the Special Investigation Squad, "My plan is to assign inspectors who show a real aptitude for detective work to the unit and relieve them of the more routine work which members of the Bureau of Inspectors normally handle." How did this description not fit Gilford and Sanders? The answer remains unclear.

WITH THE CASE FILES still sealed, it's difficult to build a reliable profile of a possible killer—however, there is useful, if limited, information. As some killers carefully select their victims, profilers also chip away at the mountain of potential suspects and create a picture of a person capable of taking a life.

That the Doodler employed vicious stabbing frenzies is a key point. Stabbing (like strangulation) is an extremely intimate form of murder. Both necessitate proximity between killer and victim, and the killer's preference for this closeness shows his need to kill in the most physical sense; simply sniping a victim from a rooftop would not be enough for him. There was an overpowering rage inside him—one that required his own hands to draw blood.

There are so few known (or suspected) serial killers within the gay community, they make up just a few pages in most textbooks on the general subject, if any. With that being said, some are the most famous of them all, such as Jeffrey Dahmer, John Wayne Gacy (also known as the Clown Killer), Wayne Williams, and Henry Lee Lucas. All but Lucas preyed solely on men and boys, with Dahmer employing some of the most gruesome torture tactics known to law enforcement. The murders by the Doodler involved blitz attacks; there was no rape, no confinement, no horrific medical experiments. When it comes to the Doodler, though, one serial killer appears to potentially share some similarities: Juan Chavez of California.

Captured in 1994 following a kidnapping in Northern California, Chavez was given two life sentences for the crime. He remarked afterward that if law enforcement thought he was dangerous because of his current conviction, they should be far more afraid of his previous crimes—serial murders. A twenty-nine-year-old Mexican immigrant, Chavez eventually confessed from Folsom State Prison to the murders of six white, middle-aged men whom he hunted in MacArthur Park in Los Angeles. Chavez lured his victims away from gay districts of the city and strangled them once they were undressed. During questioning, Chavez blamed his victims for their own deaths, as they were gay and "spreading AIDS." Just as Chavez confessed to law enforcement, the Doodler had blamed his victims for their own deaths, telling them, "You people are all the same," and boasting of murdering gay men.

Unlike what is publicly known of the Doodler, Chavez included theft in his murders, either after his victims were dead or before, when he would force them to provide their ATM personal identification numbers. While this is atypical for serial killers (particularly because Chavez would additionally steal items such as VCRs and television sets), at the center of his motivation was rage, not property theft. Dr. Eric W. Hickey, dean of the California School of Forensic Studies at Alliant International University, wrote of his interview with Chavez, "Juan appears soft-spoken, reflective, and very controlled. As I sat at a small table across from the defendant in a super-maximum-security prison, Chavez was clearly agitated. He said he really did not know why he killed his victims, but believed the 'devil made me do it.'" Hickey, who oversaw the development of the largest forensic studies program in the United States (manifested in the California School of Forensic Studies), noted that unlike other serial killers he met, Chavez was clearly depressed. But just because he was sad didn't mean he wasn't lethal. As Hickey put it, "The eyes were those of a man in horrible pain, a man living in hell. These were not the eyes one would ever wish to encounter alone."

The seed from which Chavez's murderous personality grew, he claimed, came from severe abuse by his mother and grandmother. When challenged about why he would not then murder women (as most serial killers with similar backgrounds do), he simply replied, "I came out of a woman." Perhaps more curiously, he also claimed to deeply respect women.

Chavez was an enigma, much as the Doodler was in the 1970s. Did they share anything in common?

Chapter 14

THE ARRESTS

etectives Gilford and Sanders were not originally assigned to any of the Doodler Murders until Navy hero Frederick Capin's body was found on May 12, 1975. Until then, Gerald, Jae, and Klaus's killer was hunted by a hodgepodge of homicide detectives—but it didn't take long for the handoff to Gilford and Sanders.

The murders of both Klaus Christmann and Harald Gullberg—the third and fifth known Doodler victims, respectively—were first investigated by Inspector Dave Toschi (pronounced "toss-key"). Frederick Capin's death occurred between Klaus's and Harald's, and the investigation into Capin's death began with Gilford and Sanders. Toschi went on to become one of the most notorious figures in SFPD history, as his first homicide case was the murder of twenty-nine-year-old cab driver Paul Stine by the Zodiac. The investigation launched Toschi's career into the stratosphere, with the press as his primary backer. Before Gilford and Sanders were handed Klaus's case, Toschi had worked to curate his reputation to include accolades for his relationship, albeit a somewhat romanticized version of it, with the city's gay community.

According to Toschi, he worked diligently to accumulate enough evidence and public testimony to put killers of gay men behind bars. He was not short on opportunities. Toschi frequently pointed to the same hurdle Gilford and Sanders would attempt to overcome shortly thereafter: members of the LGBTQ community had to protect their identities, and therefore, many limited their participation in police inquiries. While this problem is a known

Inspector Dave Toschi in his office at the Hall of Justice in San Francisco in 1976. *Photo by Nancy Wong. Courtesy of Wikimedia Commons.*

fact, was it the sole reason why these cases couldn't be solved? What about Melissa Honrath, who had minimal contact with the SFPD during the investigation of the murder of her brother, Jae Stevens, even though she made herself readily available for questioning?

THE DECEMBER 3, 1976 murder of fifty-year-old Richard Wilson in his Pacific Heights apartment was a case Dave Toschi wanted to get right. He, along with the rest of the SFPD, had grown tired of critiques of their homicide work—it was time for a swift arrest and subsequent praise from the press.

Wilson, the CEO and chairman of the board at Endurance Metal Products Co. in South San Francisco, was found five days after his death, lying facedown on his bed fully clothed, bound, and gagged with neckties. He had been shot in the chest and head at close range with a small-caliber gun.

Wilson's home was neat and tidy; there was no sign of forced entry or robbery. Police theorized Wilson knew his killer—that he had let him into his apartment willingly. Though his home looked as if it was in perfect condition, one of Wilson's most expensive belongings had gone missing: his brand-new 1977 dark blue Cadillac with a red interior. Police immediately put out an all-points bulletin for the vehicle and its license plate. It was their first, and only, major clue.

It didn't take long to find Wilson's car. Police from the Southern California city of El Segundo were in the Watts neighborhood of Los Angeles to serve a narcotics offense warrant when they spotted the Cadillac. They ran the plates—and got a match. Officers approached the car with guns drawn. Inside sat two men: twenty-eight-year-old Charles F. Vann and twenty-two-year-old Lawrence Robinson. Toschi immediately got on a plane alongside Inspector Hobart Nelson and headed south.

Down in Los Angeles, the two detectives interrogated Vann and Robinson. After four hours, Vann was released; Toschi felt confident he wasn't involved. He decided Robinson, who had some of Wilson's credit cards in his possession, was the sole perpetrator. Toschi and Nelson returned to the airport with Robinson in tow, eager to make their case to the district attorney—and the press.

In addition to the arrest announcement, Toschi emphasized his partnership with Gilford and Sanders on potential connections with other murders of gay men. Robinson, though arrested in Los Angeles, had practically split his time between the Bay Area and Southern California—could there be a connection between him and other murders? When Robinson's booking photo ran in the *San Francisco Sentinel*, a shiver went up the spine of many a reader. His face was a near perfect match with the 1975 composite sketch of the Doodler. Could they be one and the same?

ROBINSON'S ARREST COINCIDED WITH those of not one but four killers within San Francisco's gay community. On January 6, 1977, Gilford and Sanders apprehended twenty-four-year-old Jacob Henry Stevens, a local sex worker, for the murder of fifty-year-old actor and model Bill Wenger in his San Francisco apartment on August 29, 1976. Wenger's head and chest had been crushed by a fifty-pound glass lamp that once stood on his bedside table. After Stevens's apprehension, he confessed that he met Wenger at Lafayette Park the day of the murder and the two left the area to have sex at Wenger's apartment. A neighbor testified that around the time of Wenger's death, he heard a voice yell out, "I'm going to give it to you, Mary!" Stevens told police Wenger had said those words and that he subsequently snapped and bludgeoned his client with the lamp. Anonymous sources told the press, "Stevens had been in and out of mental institutions on a number of occasions."

Regardless of his mental state, Stevens was coherent enough to know he needed an alibi, and quick—but he was no criminal mastermind. After Wenger's murder, Stevens robbed a Larkin Street dry-cleaning shop, then promptly turned himself in. Had he not taken this extra step to cover his tracks, it's quite possible Stevens would have avoided murder charges altogether. The SFPD's crime lab had carefully collected fingerprints from Wenger's apartment. When Stevens turned himself in, he provided them with a match.

Gilford and Sanders commended Inspector Ken Moses for his fingerprint analysis, and the praise was returned by both Moses and the rest of the SFPD when details of their investigation came out. Gilford and Sanders had noticed clothing at Wenger's apartment that didn't seem to belong to him— clothing with laundry tags attached. The denim shirt and pants belonged to Stevens. He later pleaded guilty to voluntary manslaughter.

Within days of Robinson's arrest, twenty-nine-year-old Gary Myskiw and twenty-five-year-old Roderick Vanderwall were picked up by the SFPD for the brutal murder of seventy-two-year-old William Locke. While Locke's apartment at 460 Ellis Street had been ransacked and his car stolen, Myskiw and Vanderwall were motivated by more than robbery. The victim was bludgeoned, most likely with the pressure cooker found in the kitchen alongside his body. Locke was bound and handcuffed, and police implied that he was dressed in attire that suggested consent to both activities. It was not a quick death. Evidence showed Myskiw and Vanderwall revived Locke with water at some point, only to then administer a final, fatal beating.

Myskiw and Vanderwall were no Bonnie and Clyde. Within six hours of the discovery of Locke's body, the two were seated across from Inspectors Mike Mullane and John McKenna of the SFPD homicide unit. Following the murder, the pair had strolled into an Emporium department store alongside an unidentified woman. Geraldine Martin, a security officer, immediately noticed their strange demeanor as they wandered the aisles and stared at merchandise. When Myskiw and Vanderwall tried to purchase a pair of shoes, Martin walked the receipt to an upstairs office and requested a verification of the signature provided for the sale. It wasn't a match. Martin called the police.

Days after Gilford and Sanders arrested Jacob H. Stevens for the murder of Bill Wenger, Inspectors Eugene Fogarty and Frank McCoy closed in on thirty-seven-year-old Patrick Henry Ninnes, alias Michael Ruppert, on January 11, 1977. Ninnes had murdered not one but two men in San Francisco in 1975 and 1976. First was forty-five-year-old bartender Artis Harris, found bludgeoned in his Cole Street apartment on October 1, 1975. Almost a year later, on September 27, 1976, Ninnes murdered sixty-two-year-old Charles "Will" Dewing, a retired news reporter who previously lived with Ninnes. The two had had an argument prior to Dewing's murder, and Ninnes had moved out. When they met again, Dewing threatened to reveal to authorities that Ninnes's new roommate was an illegal immigrant from Canada unless Ninnes moved back in with him. To police, that was the motivation behind Dewing's brutal murder—he was both stabbed and bludgeoned repeatedly. When Dewing's body was found, one of his former roommates tipped off the SFPD and pointed to Ninnes as a potential suspect.

THE DECEMBER 16, 1976 edition of the *San Francisco Sentinel* featured the arrests of Robinson, Myskiw, and Stevens on its front page. Reporter Charles Lee wrote the article and included a separate special report in the same *Sentinel* issue under the headline "Gay Murders Defy Statistics." The piece included an interview with Lieutenant Dan Murphy, then the chief of the SFPD homicide unit.

When questioned about the lack of arrests in many murders of gay men, Murphy first pointed to a slew of criminal statistics. He cited key differences in homicide evidence: most gay victims in the city were not killed with a firearm, whereas 66 percent of other victims at the time were; while less than 16 percent of other homicides were committed with knives, more than three in five gay victims were stabbed to death; 76 percent of all murder victims knew their killer, but Murphy claimed there were no cases of gay murders in the city committed by a family member and very few gay victims who were killed by a friend. While Murphy did not provide the source of these statistics, they illustrate the parameters he placed on homicide investigations involving gay victims.

There was one hurdle Murphy pointed to as the major obstruction to justice in these cases: lack of cooperation from witnesses and other informants. As in many other SFPD press interviews, Murphy seemed incapable of recognizing this as a

San Francisco Sentinel.

consequence of decades of police abuse toward the LGBTQ community. As he put it to Charles Lee in the *Sentinel*,

> *People generally don't want to get "involved" in situations. But it seems that with the gay-related murders it's more of a problem. We get less information, dialogue, and feedback from the gay community. The reasons why are not clear. I've heard one reason or excuse given is that the police don't care and that the homicide section isn't going to put forth an effort on the gay murders. This is so totally untrue. Totally untrue....I think part of it comes from old attitudes perhaps. Towards police and by the police. Years ago, some social phenomena were less understood than they are today.*

Lee asked if Murphy was referring specifically to the gay community. "That's right. I'd say that in San Francisco we have a much more progressive attitude than many, many other major cities." When asked if he had seen a change within the SFPD regarding discrimination, Murphy replied, "Oh, definitely. I like to think that change has come about more as a step towards professionalism than anything else. We don't differentiate between victims of crime because of their sexual preference. I sincerely mean that."

Lee wasn't satisfied with Murphy's answers thus far. "Years ago, the police department kept extensive intelligence files on the gay community. Do you think gay people are not coming forward because they are afraid their names are going to get out?" Lee pressed. Murphy held fast to a certain level of dismissal. "Those fears could still be present in the community. However, I do not feel they are justified," he flatly replied.

Lee wanted an on-the-record commitment. "What assurance can you give gay people that their names won't be forwarded to the Intelligence Unit or the FBI? And have those organizations asked for any information that has turned up in the gay murders?" he asked. Murphy replied,

> *I simply cannot speak for the former command. And I'm not inferring in any way that it was different. To my knowledge no names have been forwarded to either Intelligence or the FBI. And I think I can speak for my superiors and say that it just will not happen. It's not the way we operate. We have to maintain the confidentiality of people providing us with information or we lose our effectiveness.*

Lee wrapped up his interview by referencing the arrests of Robinson, Myskiw, and Vanderwall as featured on the *Sentinel*'s front page. Would their capture push the public to ease up on its criticism of the SFPD? Rather than directly quoting Murphy, Lee wrote, "[He] responded that it would hopefully build confidence in that the Homicide Detail is indeed working on the gay murders and might encourage more people to come forward with information." Lee ended his piece with the line, "The Gay community suffers the most from its own silence about these murders."

Chapter 15

DARK HISTORY

dentifying serial killers has become a fully functioning industry since the 1990s. From television documentaries to books, podcasts, dramatizations, and more, versions of the techniques originally outlined by the FBI's Behavioral Science Unit (now called the Behavioral Analysis Unit) have been laid out for an audience of millions to study. There is, however, a notable dividing line.

Much of the hard data on psychological profiling comes from studies conducted by psychiatrists, psychologists, biopsychologists, and neuroscientists. These professions starkly differ from those in law enforcement. This is why, since the late 1980s, a number of FBI profilers have written books on their own processes, and these serve to provide a deeper look into the actual methods employed when investigating an open case.

Evidence from both law enforcement and scientific studies supports the theory that serial killers require a combination of specific characteristics and experiences in order to be shaped into lethal beings. The first is a sense of rejection during childhood. While many serial killers also experience physical abuse, it is the emotional sense of rejection and the effects of attachment deprivation that are far more impactful on the shaping of personality. Most describe themselves as loners or outcasts, shut out from society as they grew older. However, countless people could say this describes their own childhoods, and nearly none of them are serial killers. Much more is required.

A second aspect of a serial killer's development is one completely out of his* hands: genetics. While illnesses such as schizophrenia and epilepsy were once regarded as psychological disorders, they were eventually recognized as neurological diseases, and the Human Genome Project (begun in 1990 and completed in 2003) discovered combinations of genes that can make people more susceptible to these conditions. While those who suffer from these illnesses are no more violent than the overall population, this is another recurring element in many serial killers' development when present with the other key factors. Additionally, there have been several notable court cases involving a defense that presents past head trauma as evidence of technical innocence. Like the other aforementioned traits, head trauma is indeed an important factor but cannot stand alone as an explanation for a killer's actions.

The third aspect of a serial killer's development is grounded in his trigger experiences. Examples would be the loss of a job, a divorce, or the death of a loved one. These triggers can also be more minor: an argument with a friend or a passing comment from a stranger. Whatever they might be, these events trigger a psychological explosion in a serial killer that sets in motion the murders he has been contemplating for quite some time. For some, this detonation of the psyche means immediately hitting the streets in search of a victim. For others, it can serve as the starting point for intricate preplanning that can last months, or even years. For the planners, an additional trigger event often occurs just prior to a murder. Some stalk a victim for weeks or months, others choose a random house to invade—and one would blend into the shadows of San Francisco's shoreline, feet in the sand, matching his stride to the one he would kill.

OVERSEEN BY THE FBI's Behavioral Analysis Unit, the National Center for the Analysis of Violent Crime serves as a resource for local and state jurisdictions in search of assistance with crimes not automatically referred to the FBI. Most notably, the NCAVC (as it is commonly known) provides a wealth of experience backed by hard data for police departments to employ in their own investigations.

In 2014, the center released a fairly thorough manual titled *Serial Murder: Pathways for Investigations*. The report is compiled from five years of research, and a foreword notes that much of what the reader will learn

---

* The pronouns used in this book when referencing unnamed serial killers are he/him, as 98 percent of known serial killers are male.

is in direct contrast with previous publications by both the FBI and some of its former members. Those prior publications and the theories they present were brought to audiences worldwide when Netflix released the series *Mindhunter* in 2017. The show is based on the 1995 book of the same name, written by John Douglas, who is considered by many to be the father of serial killer profiling.

By Douglas's account, profiling often involves a profound deductive ability—the tiniest, most overlooked clues can reveal the killer's psyche and lead to his arrest. Douglas's theories are not unfounded—in fact, it was he, alongside fellow agent Robert Ressler, who was instrumental in starting the Behavioral Science Unit in the first place. The foreword to *Pathways for Investigations*, however, makes clear that new data acquired from new subjects through new methods presents key differences from past research, including Douglas and Ressler's. It states, in part:

> *Although a multitude of information has been published relating to serial murder, most of the studies were conducted from the perspective of an identified offender and concentrated on the offender's development; upbringing; familial relationships; history of physical, sexual, and emotional abuse; and other factors, which were viewed in terms of causality. A number of these studies, including the FBI's original study, also relied on self-reported information obtained from offenders during interviews.*

The NCAVC found that these research methods were not helpful to law enforcement when searching for potential suspects in an active investigation, since those hauled in for questioning do not typically share the deepest, darkest parts of their childhoods with detectives.

Additionally, police are legally prohibited from accessing medical and psychological records—therefore, building a profile of a killer that is reliant on his projected psyche, no matter how spot-on that profile might be, is irrelevant if it cannot help achieve its own objective: narrowing down the list of suspects. The NCAVC study presents its five years of research as a tool to alternatively approach a serial murder investigation; rather than focus on psychological components, the researchers collected data that "was substantial enough to allow the authors to search frequencies and common occurrences between [four factors:] the body disposal scenario, other behaviors at the crime scene, the criminal history of the offender, and the relationship between the offender and the victim." This does not equate to a formulaic outline for serial killer development; outlier killers were also included in the study—such as what the FBI refers to as "serial same-sex murderers," as the Doodler is classified.

The study involved a total of ninety-two offenders, seven of whom fell into the "serial same-sex murderer" category. While data on only seven subjects was obtained, these seven alone were responsible for the murders of sixty-eight men. Most of the victims (63.2 percent) were between fourteen and twenty-nine years of age; 50 percent of them were Black, 39.7 percent were white, and 10.2 percent were of various other ethnicities.

When it came to perpetrators, 57.1 percent were white, and 42.9 percent were Black*; no other ethnicities are noted in the sample group. Most subjects in the study were between eighteen and thirty-five years of age when they committed their first murders. One killer was married; the majority were dependent on either family or another outside resource. Most had completed at least high school, and others had furthered their education. It is notable, though, that even with these achievements, less than half of the sample group was employed. Two of the killers previously served in the military. Most had a previous arrest, with the majority of offenses listed as sexual assault and driving while under the influence. Less than half had been diagnosed with a mental illness before they began their series of murders.

So, how does this data square with what is known of the Doodler? A comparison of facts shows him to be an outlier in some respects while also fitting snugly within the confines of known statistics. His choice of victims fits within the parameters of the study pool. That his known murder sites were not in his home, his car, or the victim's home is more unique. The locations of his attacks on his surviving victims (their apartments) is a more common factor. The age when he began his murders (approximately nineteen to twenty-one) is a commonality shared with the entire sample group. With only 2.9 percent of the studied murders perpetrated by stabbing, the Doodler lies within the narrowest margin in the range of modus operandi.

The "same-sex serial murderer" portion of the NCAVC study included data on only seven offenders; there is an overall lack of academic studies on the subject. As for the number of participants, when it comes to the overall number of known serial killers, those who fall into the "same-sex" category are few and far between.

---

* Black Americans are incarcerated in state prisons at nearly five times the rate of white Americans; they are overrepresented in the vast majority of criminal research due to centuries of racial bias.

THAT THE DOODLER WAS allegedly a Black male has been a hurdle to investigators both then and now, because the fact is, this killer's demographic is extremely under-researched. On the rare occasion it is analyzed, it is almost exclusively through scholarly articles written by researchers who are not representative of their case study subjects. The inherent bias is something serious investigators cannot ignore. One man, however, has contributed landmark work on the subject.

Dr. Allan Branson is a graduate of the FBI National Academy and a twenty-six-year law enforcement veteran. Now a member of the American Psychological Association and a criminal justice professor at Arcadia University, he has spent years researching and publishing data on Black serial killers. He is also the author of *The Anonymity of African American Serial Killers: A Continuum of Negative Imagery from Slavery to Prisons*—a vital publication on the study of Black serial killers, written by a Black researcher.

Dr. Branson contends the lack of research in this field is grounded in America's long history of the assumption of violence in Black men. White serial killers are often depicted as guy-next-door figures; acquaintances and strangers often attest to the killer as being "seemingly normal." Their reigns of terror are a shock to the public, shaking citizens who fear that "safe" people can seethe with rage beneath the surface. Coverage of Black serial killers is much scanter; their stories are presented as much less intriguing— whether an audience realizes it or not, the deeply embedded portrayal of the Black man as an inherently violent figure throughout the history of America lies at the root of these narratives.

While some theorize the lack of coverage is due to a concern for political correctness, this idea doesn't pan out in the bigger picture, especially when it comes to news and entertainment. Reporters regularly cover instances of Black violence when it fits a neatly framed stereotype—crimes such as robbery and gang shootings. Most serial killers, even when the facts don't fit the bill, are portrayed as highly intelligent and calculating—even ingenious. This depiction doesn't square with the centuries-old trope that has existed since the days of slavery, and so Black serial killers are almost always overlooked not only by the public but by researchers as well. Perhaps the best example of this would be Samuel Little, a man well known in serious true crime circles but far from a household name. Men like Ted Bundy, Jeffrey Dahmer, and Charles Manson are infamous in American history; their names are sealed tightly in the minds of the public—their faces even printed on darkly humorous T-shirts. The highest body count between the three lies with Bundy, who killed thirty-six women. The lowest goes to Manson, who (technically) killed no one. Yet Samuel Little, a Black serial killer, was confirmed by the FBI to have been involved in at least sixty murders; he has confessed to ninety-three.

Based on the details available to the public, including the accusations made against the psychiatric patient reported by Dr. Priest, Dr. Branson has built a partial profile of the man police dubbed the Doodler. By taking the threads of what we do know in order to form theories on what we don't, Dr. Branson provides a picture of an educated and emotionally complex man whose troubled childhood and self-hatred formed him into a dedicated killer.

Chapter 16

KILLER'S BREW

The childhood of every well-documented serial killer is filled with deeply negative experiences, one of which surfaces eerily throughout research—including that of the NCAVC. This is not the presence of violence but rather a deprivation of affection by one or both parents. Often, this deprivation morphs into outright hostility, and Dr. Branson believes this to be the case with the Doodler.

By piecing together the limited details available, Dr. Branson posits that the killer experienced a life of rejection. The focus on gay male victims most likely came from his own attractions, as also theorized by Gilford and Sanders. These attractions are potentially a partial source of the lack of connection he experienced with one or both parental figures. As Dr. Branson put it to this writer, "It always goes back to the family structure. It's the only structure you know, and it becomes the microcosm of the world you're about to enter into." In the case of the Doodler, the killer's feelings of alienation might have manifested themselves in what is called the Macdonald Triad—a set of three factors highly consistent in the childhood development of serial killers. The theory was first developed by psychiatrist J.M. Macdonald and published in a 1963 article in the *American Journal of Psychiatry* but has remained relevant in the decades that followed. The three factors are arson, cruelty to animals, and enuresis (commonly known as bedwetting). Dr. Branson pointed out that with regard to bedwetting, it is not the act of urination but the humiliation that occurs afterward that can immensely impact a child. Most often, at least two of the three factors are present in a serial killer's history. Dr. Branson noted that aside from arson, the Doodler very likely had a history of other peripheral offenses, such as robbery and assault. This would also correlate with data collected in the NCAVC's *Pathways for Investigations* report.

If the Doodler was truly a budding artist, Dr. Branson theorized that he led a life deeply imbedded in fantasy and sought refuge from his intrapsychic conflict in creativity. "Every time he draws, it's a fantasy," as Dr. Branson put it. Possibly an only child, the Doodler spent much of his time alone, falling deeper into his inner world to escape a tormented reality. While he potentially morphed into what is called a "missionary killer" (someone seeking to rid the world of a specific demographic, such as gay men—like Juan Chavez), he much more likely struggled with his own sexual identity, and the murders were born out of that internal conflict.

Many sources of psychological research on Black sexual identity, Dr. Branson pointed out, are inherently flawed. Freud, for example, he considers mostly irrelevant when it comes to the subject: "Freud explored sexuality of a Victorian age—does that relate to African Americans that were also living in that age? You have to look at the cultural aspects of the situation." In January 1976, Detective Gilford also addressed the unique struggles of gay Black men in the '70s, telling *San Francisco Chronicle* journalist Maitland Zane, "Homosexuality has never been accepted by the Black community.…The guilt he is experiencing causes him to want to erase the acts he's committed." In December the following year, though, Gilford's quote would be countered by a major milestone when Lieutenant Governor Mervyn Dymally, the highest-ranking Black politician in California, served as the featured speaker at a dinner honoring Harvey Milk. During the event, Milk said, "It is more than just symbolic to have Blacks and gays standing together and supporting each other—it shows how far the gay movement has advanced in a relatively few years. It shows the potential all minorities have."

When it comes to subjects studied in psychological reports as a whole, Dr. Branson noted that the extreme lack of representation of Black men is often due to their justified avoidance of participation. He reflected on a key question therapy patients ask themselves: "Does the psychologist look like me?" Again, it is the lack of representation within psychological institutions that obstructs those institutions' very research. The lack of solid data is directly connected with the failure of many FBI profilers when building a picture of a Black serial killer. "Where the FBI screwed up was with ethnocentric profiles. When you do that, you leave yourself open, which is why it took so long to catch the D.C. snipers," said Dr. Branson.* One key question in Dr. Branson's profiling process is whether or not deception or physical confrontation was used when ensnaring victims. In the Doodler case, it was the former. Dr. Branson deduced, "He was successful because not only is his artwork good—it's also that he's charming....He's in control when this is happening. He needs to be in order for victims to lower their defenses. Psychopathic people can compartmentalize; he doesn't do a lot of hand-wringing when this is over."

Despite several news reports in the 1970s to the contrary, none of the Doodler victims' autopsies showed any signs of sexual assault or activity, though Klaus, Frederick, and Harald were found with their pants unzipped— and in Harald's case, his underwear was likely removed. The absence of any physical evidence of sexual activity in all of the known victims' autopsies can indicate many things—and potentially be of vital importance when building a profile of the killer. Firstly, while he might not have had physical contact with the victims' bodies in a sexual way, that does not exclude a wide range of other possibilities. There are numerous cases of masturbatory behavior immediately following a murder by a serial killer. Many such killers do not leave evidence on the victims' bodies. No details are available on any physical evidence collected at the crime scenes, so the possibility that signs of sexual activity were found on the victims' clothing or elsewhere at the scene cannot be eliminated.

While most serial killers commit sexual assault during their murders, these acts are not a requirement when defining sexually motivated homicides. With or without sexual assault, the overwhelming majority of serial killers share common ground through the sexual motivation factor. The Doodler's sexual motivation is exhibited through his use of seduction prior to his murders. When it comes to the lack of sexual assault in those killings, Dr. Branson pointed to piquerism, the act of arousal through repeatedly stabbing a victim. In this circumstance, the knife serves as a phallic object to the killer, rather than his own body: "If you found evidence of sexual action, that could cancel out the cause of the crimes, which is self-hatred."

---

* The D.C. sniper attacks (also known as the Beltway sniper attacks) were a series of coordinated shootings that occurred over three weeks in October 2002 in the District of Columbia, Maryland, and Virginia. Ten people were killed and three others were critically wounded in the Baltimore–Washington metropolitan area and along Interstate 95 in Virginia. The snipers were forty-one-year-old John Allen Muhammad and seventeen-year-old Lee Boyd Malvo. Their crimes included murders and robberies in the states of Alabama, Arizona, Florida, Georgia, Louisiana, and Texas and in Washington, D.C. By the time they were apprehended on October 24, 2002, Muhammad and Malvo had killed seventeen people and wounded ten others.

After reviewing Gerald Cavanagh's autopsy, Dr. Branson noticed the potential use of not one but *two* knives during his murder. This possible discovery supports the theory that this was the Doodler's first kill as, to Dr. Branson, it indicates a lack of both confidence and experience. In addition, Ocean Beach protected the killer from potential witnesses with the roar of the sea and the fog cloaking the night. "He had to be familiar with that area in order to pull it off.…The beach is a good place to further the deception. It seems romantic and then explodes," said Dr. Branson.

The thefts of victims' identification and other items on their person doesn't indicate to Dr. Branson that robbery was a motive; rather, they served to both delay police and add to a collection of trophies that allowed the killer to "savor and relive" the murders in his mind. This is very common with serial killers in general and, many times, has served as their downfall, as trophies are indisputable evidence of involvement.

When it comes to the tip provided by an unidentified person about the Zebra Murders that read "Zebra, [name redacted], Polk St., Black, Makeup, Gay," Dr. Branson doubts it is related. Detective Earl Sanders shared the same opinion with writer Bennett Cohen while the two were collaborating on the book *The Zebra Murders: A Season of Killing, Racial Madness, and Civil Rights*. The number of seemingly relevant tips provided to Gilford and Sanders during the Zebra investigation was staggering—and 99 percent resulted in wasted man hours and dead ends. Still, no one can be sure.

That Harald Gullberg's blue windbreaker was removed prior to his killing and then replaced afterward could mean several things. It is possible this indicated a level of shame within the killer or, more likely, was an effective effort to delay the discovery of Harald's decayed body. Lands End was known as a haven for the homeless, and it's possible several people glanced at a dead Harald, thinking he had fallen into a drunken slumber.

With regard to the man who was reported by a psychiatrist and brought in for questioning on multiple occasions, Dr. Branson knows that even if the police have collected and preserved crime scene DNA, a sample from the patient would have to be provided voluntarily in order to test for a match. Additionally, it's very likely that any remaining DNA has deteriorated due to improper storage. DNA fingerprinting was first used in a police investigation in 1986, well after the Doodler's known murders occurred, and proper storage procedures were completely unknown to law enforcement at the time.

The killer's victims shared key similarities: all were white, male, and gay, and several were transplants and closeted. All were sober or nearly so, with the exception of Klaus Christmann, whose blood alcohol level was recorded as 0.33 percent. Klaus's murder was the most violent of those publicly tied to the Doodler and included not one, but three ear-to-ear slashes of the throat. Dr. Branson believes there is a link between the increased viciousness of the attack and the fact Klaus was heavily intoxicated: "He may prefer his victims sober so that they are conscious of death, as it gives him more of a feeling of power and control."

In reference to the fact that Gerald, Klaus, Frederick, and Harald were immigrants and did not have a solid foundation of friends and family in San Francisco, Dr. Branson noted serial killers often target members of society who are unlikely to be immediately missed. "When a victim belongs to a family and has agency, that's usually the killer's downfall."

Chapter 17

IT'S ALL A GAME

I t is impossible to fully examine the Doodler case without studying other serial killers who prowled California's gay bars and pickup spots for numerous victims in the 1970s. In 1972, two years before the Doodler's murder of Gerald Cavanagh, Randy Steven Kraft began his eleven-year reign as one of the deadliest criminals in the history of the United States.

The path that led to Kraft's yearslong murder series includes outlier elements alongside well-documented precursors to the development of serial killers. Kraft's parents were Opal and Harold Kraft; their fourth child and only son was born on March 19, 1945, into what, according to known evidence, was a generally stable and healthy family life. Three older sisters and a doting mother served to provide a nurturing environment, though Kraft's father, a production worker, was described as "distant" and minimally involved with the family's social dynamic.

The Kraft family was far from wealthy, and Opal often took on various jobs in order to provide additional money to the monthly budget. Nevertheless, she was a dedicated member of the PTA and was actively involved in Kraft's upbringing. By all known accounts, she had a kind and caring nature.

Kraft dated girls in high school, though some friends and teachers later attested to private suspicions about his sexuality. His family, however, claim they were totally unaware of his attractions. When Kraft began to bring home a string of male "friends" to meet his family while on visits from college, his parents and sisters assumed, at first, the relationships were genuinely platonic.

One passion came to consume Kraft's life at an early age: politics. A self-described "ultra-conservative Republican," Kraft campaigned for 1964 presidential candidate Barry Goldwater and asserted that his career goal was to one day serve in the Senate. Just four years later, however, he became a dedicated member of Robert F. Kennedy's campaign for the highest office in the land—so much so, he received a letter of gratitude prior to Kennedy's assassination in 1968. Before the pendulum of his political affiliations swung drastically, Kraft enrolled at Claremont Men's College in Claremont, California. He was awarded a scholarship based on his outstanding academic achievements after he graduated tenth out of 390 students at his alma mater, Westminster High School. Early into his first year at Claremont, Kraft enrolled in the Claremont Reserve Officers Training Corps and showed strong public support for the war in Vietnam. By the time his sophomore year began, Kraft had left his conservative views and the reserve behind, begun bartending at a local gay club, and started his first relationship with a man.

Kraft grew acquainted with Orange County's gay scene in the 1960s, but not without incident. Huntington Beach set the stage for Kraft's first encounter with law enforcement while cruising the restrooms and lifeguard shacks that dotted the shoreline in 1966. A junior in college, Kraft unwittingly approached a plainclothes officer for sex and landed a charge for lewd conduct. The policeman let Kraft go without a citation but issued a stern warning against any repeat incidents.

Airman Randy Steven Kraft, 1969. Defense exhibit in Kraft's trial. *Orange County Superior Court No. C52776.*

Shortly after graduating in February 1968, Kraft joined the United States Air Force. While stationed at Edwards Air Force Base in Kern County, California, Kraft supervised the painting of test planes prior to inspection by the higher-ups. While he was far from soaring skies and rapid gunfire, Kraft served the force well enough to earn the rank of Airman First Class. Following this achievement, he decided to formally notify his family that he was, in fact, gay. The truth—and Kraft—came out.

Kraft claimed to a friend that his father's reaction bordered on violent, while his mother kept calm, assuring herself that being gay was a "condition" to be cured. Eventually, the family

THE SAN FRANCISCO DOODLER MURDERS

unified behind its only son, but Kraft's sisters noticed a subtle but growing rift. Still, their brother frequently spoke to both them and their parents. And when the Kraft family later faced the ultimate test of allegiance, they stood behind him until the very end.

THERE IS NO EVIDENCE Kraft's family ever abused him, but that's not to say he didn't suffer significant physical trauma as a child. Referred to as "accident prone" in several documents, at the age of two, Kraft managed to tumble down a flight of stairs, causing a head injury that today could be classified as a Traumatic Brain Injury (or TBI). Several substantial studies have been conducted to explore a potential correlation, if not causation, between a serial killer's brain development and his lack of concern for victims' suffering. While TBIs present themselves through a huge range of physical and psychological symptoms, the overwhelming majority of those suffering from these injuries are not violent. What is provable is Kraft was medicated starting at an early age.

After coming out, Kraft began to experience severe headaches and stomach pain—common symptoms of significant stress. Kraft returned to the same doctor, Wilson C. McArthur, who saw him for his head injury as a toddler. Over the years, Dr. McArthur provided Kraft with treatment consisting of numerous painkillers and muscle relaxants. Some of these medications became Kraft's future murder accomplices, rendering his victims completely helpless prior to their deaths.

Whether Kraft's childhood wounds and medical treatments helped to create a monster is indiscernible, but he did encounter a potential trigger event during the same period. After coming out to his family, Kraft went to his Air Force supervisors in 1969 and told them he was gay. A response so swift it practically arrived on a breeze came next—a general discharge on "medical grounds." Kraft was furious. He knew the general (versus honorable) discharge would leave a stain on his record that would stand out to future employers. He consulted a lawyer without success. LGBTQ members of all military branches would have to wait until 2011 to be publicly accepted by the ranks.

Around this time, Kraft met Jeff Graves, whose drug use and sex life played a role in eventually ending the touch-and-go romance. Based on Kraft's journal entries, it is believed he began his decade-plus murder series around this time, in September 1971, with thirty-year-old victim Wayne Joseph Dukette. Dukette's badly decomposed body was found on October

5 near Ortega Highway in south Orange County. The medical examiner could not immediately determine the cause of death but signed off on a diagnosis of acute alcohol intoxication after Dukette registered a blood alcohol level of 0.36 percent. It would take over a decade for prosecutors to uncover the truth—time had hidden away the most horrifying evidence Kraft left behind.

It was quite possible Kraft even scared himself with Dukette's murder, for he waited fifteen months to find Edward Daniel Moore, a twenty-year-old Marine stationed at Camp Pendleton in San Diego County. Moore was shy but friendly and frequently down on his luck. He rarely seemed to have two pennies to rub together and traveled nearly exclusively by hitchhiking. Many a meal was provided by men Moore had charmed on the streets, but that didn't mar his authentic kindness. Months before he died, Moore began occasionally seeing Charles Wendell Vines Jr., a former second lieutenant in the Army who had moved on to help run the San Diego Military Academy. Moore confided in Vines about his alcoholic parents, his mother's death, his molestation at a foster home. Vines had plenty of trysts with younger men just looking for a place to crash, but Eddie had a sincerity about him that stood out.

After Moore's body was discovered on December 26, 1972, in the nearby city of Seal Beach, detectives made their way to Vines's door. Vines had been tossed a line by one of Moore's friends saying that he was found dead, but Vines thought it was a joke. When police showed up asking questions, reality set in. They spared no details when describing the body dump site on the 405 off-ramp. Moore was strangled to death after a brutal beating and then shoved from a moving car onto the road. A sock had been inserted into his rectum and his genitals mutilated. The detectives dropped crime scene photos on the table before Vines, one by one. The shadow of guilt they saw over him had grown into a thunderous cloud, and it would take years to dissipate.

In 1975, following his breakup with Graves, Kraft met nineteen-year-old Jeff Seelig at a party. Seelig's gruff tones and strong brow made him look and seem older. Graves had not been ready to settle down, and that led to the couple's ultimate demise. Kraft was not looking to immediately jump back into monogamy, but soon Seelig was doing all of the things partners sometimes do—even going so far as to redesign Kraft's apartment and suggest new clothes for him to wear. When they first met, Seelig told Kraft he was twenty-six, not nineteen, and for a while that worked; Seelig and Kraft began to share a home in Laguna Hills soon after, marking the start of a deeply tumultuous relationship. When Seelig's high school friends started coming around, his cover was blown. The lie about his age triggered the first of many arguments that would span nearly a decade.

To many of the couple's friends, Kraft and Seelig fell into what they considered to be a stereotypical dynamic; Kraft played the older, stabler, and slightly subdued role, while Seelig was the younger, spritelier, more sociable man of the pair. Kraft was also comfortable spending a night in with his boyfriend, while Seelig was still very much a partygoer and loved to play host as well. The pair opened their home to multiple game nights each week. Bridge was Kraft's favorite game. It was more than just fun for him, though. Despite his cool, calm, and collected demeanor during his matchups, Kraft had an internal obsession with the game—if he lost, he never forgot it. Friends later told the press he would sometimes celebrate his triumph over them in a game by referencing a loss he had suffered at their hands years prior.

Kraft's love of bridge made sense to many people in his life—his talent with numbers had grown into his livelihood, and he was now a data-processing consultant. The two skill sets seemed to go hand in hand. Phil Crabtree, a close friend of both Kraft and Seelig, later told journalist Dennis McDougal,

> *I think the first death was accidental somehow. Maybe it was intentional, but whether it was or not, it must have clicked something that made it a challenge to him: if you can get away with one, then it was almost like playing bridge. Because it didn't matter. Once you've done one, it really didn't matter if there were more. From then on, it was strictly the challenge of how clever and cunning and skillful you could be. Bridge is the same way: once you've started, you just go and go as long as you possibly can until you lose.*

When Seelig was left unsatisfied in the relationship, he often headed to a bar and left Kraft steaming on the couch—it was Kraft, after all, who had first taken Seelig to the clubs and cruising spots where he was headed. It didn't help that Seelig was into BDSM; Kraft was not and knew there were plenty of other men whom Seelig could seduce. A familiar feeling must have crept up on Kraft, for this was not the first time an unstable relationship led him to kill.

THE CASES THAT FOLLOWED were some of the most gruesome ever studied in the history of serial killer analysis. The level of torture, mutilation, and defilement inflicted by Kraft defies comprehension. Convicted of sixteen murders and likely responsible for a sixty-seven-person body count, Kraft was apprehended on May 14, 1983, in Orange County after he was pulled over by police for driving erratically. It had been over a decade since Dukette's murder. When the officers approached the car, they noticed an unresponsive passenger, who tumbled onto the ground after the door was opened.

His name was Terry Lee Gambrel, and he was dying. He was fading fast while police were administering field sobriety tests on Kraft just feet away; as was the pattern with many of Kraft's victims, Gambrel had been plied with drugs and alcohol. A combination of both had rendered him completely helpless—an ideal state for Kraft's plans to strangle him with a ligature.

Gambrel was a twenty-five-year-old Marine stationed at El Toro and was engaged to be married. When he did not show up to a housewarming party he had committed to attending, Sergeant Ronald Phillips noticed. Found on Gambrel's body were handwritten directions to the gathering, tucked safely into his pocket.

Kraft's killing grounds spanned from Southern California to Oregon and even Michigan as well, where he once attended a work seminar in Grand Rapids. He also spent time in the Bay Area during the 1970s for the same employer who sent him out of state, but he has never been charged with any Northern California murders. The geographical range of Kraft's victims and the fact that the majority have not been identified creates a needle-in-a-haystack effect, making justice a distant possibility.

What's more, Kraft didn't always follow a pattern. The sock-in-the-rectum signature was repeated several times, but not as a rule. Most victims died from strangulation, but not all. Drugs and alcohol played major roles in many of Kraft's murders, but not in every case. Many of Kraft's victims were gay or bisexual men he lured from a bar or off a street corner, but some were straight and simply hitchhiking.

The estimated total number of victims does not come from known cases but, rather, from Kraft himself. Found in his car was a notebook containing a list of sixty-one cryptic, handwritten entries. Once Kraft was brought to trial, the prosecution presented evidence that thirteen of the entries corresponded with his known California victims. The prosecution further posited that an additional eight entries documented Kraft's murders in Oregon and Michigan. Four entries included the number two, potentially indicating a double homicide. Kraft made sure these memories didn't just live in his own head—following a search warrant, photographs of victims were located in Kraft's possession. Many of these images were likely taken premortem.

Prosecuting attorneys noted that while the remaining entries could not be linked to a specific victim, they likely were. Who were the other victims on Kraft's list?

DESPITE KRAFT'S STAGGERING SAVAGERY and the overwhelming evidence presented against him, forty-four character witnesses attended his sentencing hearing. Forty-four friends, coworkers, family members, and other loved ones would stand, for the world to see, and attest to another Kraft—a different Kraft—who was a world apart from the horrific, soulless creature presented by the prosecution—or rather, Kraft's self-documentation of his own crimes. This man, in their eyes, was worth saving. This man, out of whose own car spilled a dying Terry Lee Gambrel. This man, who tortured to such a degree that one victim's eyelids were removed so as to force him to bear witness to his own end.

There was nineteen-year-old James Dale Reeves, who never made it home to his parents after they sent him off with the family car to meet his friends at a gay community church. Twenty-three-year-old Vincent Cruz Mestas's hands, the fine instruments he was tuning at Long Beach State University as an art student, were never found. Patrons of the Princess Louise restaurant never saw twenty-five-year-old server Thomas Paxton Lee flash his flirtatious smile after 1974.

Both Kraft and Seelig consistently told law enforcement Seelig had no knowledge whatsoever of Kraft's murders, and no evidence was found to contradict this. However, in several of his victims' cases, both circumstantial and DNA evidence strongly suggest Kraft had an accomplice. In a number of instances, police were unable to determine how Kraft pushed his victims from his car and closed the passenger door while simultaneously driving at a relatively high speed. Regarding the DNA, as of 2022, there has been no match to the third-party samples collected from the crime scenes. What is certain is that while Kraft still walked the streets, at least two other serial killers operated within striking distance—their stories splashed across newspaper headlines and television screens.

Randy Steven Kraft has always maintained his innocence and refuses to aid in the investigations of his other victims. His final appeal was exhausted in 2000. As of this writing, he awaits his death at San Quentin.

Chapter 18

THE ROAD KILLERS

Police were confused. At the same time the Doodler and Randy Kraft stalked California's shorelines, more bodies of gay men were popping up near roadsides. It seemed there was another, newer predator stalking the streets. In reality, Patrick Wayne Kearney had been around for some time and had simply begun showing off. From 1962 to 1977, Kearney took a minimum of twenty-one lives—a number estimated to be closer to forty-three in actuality.

Born in Los Angeles on September 24, 1939, Kearney spent much of his youth as a sickly child and grew to a meek five-foot, five-inch frame. The eldest of three sons, Kearney was an only child until his brother Michael was born four years later, with Chester, the youngest, coming into the family when Kearney was five. The boys' parents were George and Eunice Kearney, an LAPD officer and a homemaker, respectively. George, the disciplinarian of the family, later quit law enforcement in favor of a career as a salesman for a travel agency, requiring the family to move to Arizona when Kearney was in the middle of seventh grade.

The Kearney family was relatively stable but of lower-class economic status, which brought about its own stresses. While there is no solid evidence Kearney experienced abuse in his home, this was not the case at school. No matter where he was receiving his education, from California to Arizona and Texas, Kearney was relentlessly harassed and eventually came to spend his time daydreaming about murdering his bullies, starting at age eight. In the following years, Kearney selected some of his victims based on physical similarities to those who had tormented him.

At age thirteen, Kearney was taught how to slaughter pigs by his father, who purchased him a .22-caliber rifle to commemorate the occasion. Years later, it was the same tactic—a single shot behind the left ear—that Kearney used on his victims. While still a boy, he quickly became comfortable with killing animals and soon progressed to defiling their remains afterward.

Kearney's family returned to California from Arizona in time for him to finish high school in Redondo Beach. Yet almost immediately after graduation, he and his family relocated yet again to Texas. In a yo-yo fashion, Kearney moved back west to Long Beach shortly thereafter and registered for the Air Force at age nineteen. He wanted to travel the globe and put to use his fluency in Spanish, Japanese, and Chinese. Instead, an ironic twist of fate would land him stationed back in Texas yet again. It was there he met David Hill.

HILL WAS BORN THE seventh of nine children in Lubbock, Texas, on Christmas Eve 1942. Unlike Kearney, Hill stood at six foot two and had a muscular frame. The two started their turbulent fifteen-year romance shortly after meeting in the Air Force in 1960. Hill had married his high school sweetheart, Linda Gayle, then divorced her prior to moving into Kearney's Long Beach, California apartment. Kearney had been honorably discharged from the Air Force and returned to the Golden State for good. The relationship between Hill and Kearney was rocky at best, with Hill returning to Texas not only to reunite with Linda but also to father a child with her. It was during that period in 1962 that Kearney killed his first known victims.

Kearney began his foray into the gay community on both sides of the Mexican border, picking up men from San Diego to Tijuana. He loved Mexican culture, and his fluency in Spanish helped him explore it to the fullest. On many of his long drives south, he committed his murders along the way. His first victims were picked up alongside of the road, in search of a ride. As Kearney grew in confidence, he began cruising gay bars and hookup spots to select men to kill.

Sometime during spring of that year, while Hill was in Texas with Linda Gayle, Kearney picked up a still-unidentified nineteen-year-old man in Indio, California. The victim had been hitchhiking. After Kearney shot the John Doe in the head, he had sex with the body, mutilated it, and left it beside Highway 86.

Kearney later claimed that his second victim was the cousin of his first; he had witnessed Kearney pick up the John Doe, and Kearney needed to cover his tracks. The cousin was brought to the same location and faced the same fate. There was a third victim in 1962, an eighteen-year-old man known to Kearney and law enforcement only as "Mike."

After abandoning his child and Linda Gayle for a second and final time, Hill returned to Kearney, and the relationship picked up where it left off in California. Kearney began making an impressive salary as a senior research assistant at Hughes Aircraft, and in 1964, the couple relocated to Culver City.

Hill, on the other hand, wasn't working and relied solely on Kearney's income. Resentment and acrimony brewed within their partnership, and Kearney often took off for drives south to Tijuana. In June 1971, he found a note from Hill telling him the relationship was done for good. Kearney snapped and left a trail of bodies in his wake.

THE WAY BOTH KEARNEY and Hill later told it to law enforcement, the pair would have heated arguments and separate. During these periods, both men said Kearney would go "on long drives" to find, kill, and dump his victims— unbeknownst to Hill. According to Kearney, Hill had zero knowledge of these activities and never participated.

After all, Hill had broken up with Kearney and was back in Texas with Linda Gayle when Kearney had last lost control. There was a lull in his murders between 1962 and December 1967, when he and Hill separated again. Kearney lured a man he only remembers as "George" back to his house from a local gay bar. The two had barely made it through the front door when Kearney shot George in the head, killing him instantly. Kearney had sex with the body before dragging it to a bathtub in the house, skinning, and dismembering it.

George lay buried in the backyard for a decade. On July 8, 1977, law enforcement followed Kearney's hand-drawn map to the unmarked grave, where they dug up the corpse and officially added George to Kearney's growing list of victims.

IT WAS A FEW years after George's murder, in June 1971, when Hill left that devastating note for Kraft and walked out the door. Just a few days later, thirteen-year-old John Demchik was hitchhiking in Inglewood when Kearney picked him up. He was not the first, nor the youngest, of Kearney's victims between 1971 and 1977, when he was finally apprehended.

Kearney also preyed on gay sex workers, such as twenty-one-year-old Albert Rivera, who died at Kearney's hand in San Diego. He knew these victims would buy him some time, as their transient nature made their absences less likely to be noticed. Many victims' bodies were never found, and their existence is known only due to Kearney's confessions.

In Rivera's case, his body was found on April 13, 1975, shortly after he was murdered. His fate had been nearly identical to George's; he was brought back to Kearney's Culver City home, shot in the head, defiled, taken to a bathtub, and dismembered. This time, however, Kearney didn't conceal the body in his own backyard. Rivera's body, piece by piece, was scattered throughout Los Angeles in trash bags. One of them, left near State Highway 74, was noticed by a passerby just hours after Rivera was killed.

It was the use of trash bags in many of his murders that caught the ear of the press. By 1975, the horribly mutilated bodies of Randy Kraft's victims had been showing up for years, but this was different. These bodies had been dismembered and showed all the signs of necrophilia, and none had been tortured premortem. A single shot to the head seemed to be a signature; the other bodies bore horrific wounds suffered while they were still alive. Kearney was not the man torturing his victims prior to their deaths—and Kraft was not the only man who was.

KEARNEY DID NOT LIMIT his victims to grown men. On August 24, 1974, Kearney found five-year-old Ronald Dean Smith Jr. heading back to his Lennox, California home after playing in a nearby park. He was due for dinner. His grandmother Shirley O'Conner had volunteered to watch him while his mother was away on a trip to Washington and Oregon. He never showed. Shirley searched the neighborhood. She found a friend Ronald had been playing with, safe and sound. But Ronald had vanished. She rushed home and called the LAPD. Before the authorities could locate Joann O'Connor, Ronald's mother, his disappearance was already on the front page of the local newspaper. Over forty deputies searched Ronald's neighborhood door by door but turned up nothing. Joann's estranged husband, Ronald Sr., joined the search. Nothing was found.

A week later, and Ronald was still missing. Joann, grief-stricken, spent her twenty-third birthday meeting with the press, pleading through sobs to Ronald's captor for his return. Her statement, begun with a whisper that grew into a wail, reads in part,

He's a good little boy, a sensitive child who gets upset when someone squashes a bug. When I'm upset or crying, he'll wash my tears and he'll come up and hug me....I don't know what you want me to do. Please, oh, please! Tell me what you want me to do!

Forty-nine days later, Ronald's body was found by teenagers collecting beer cans near Lake Elsinore, a city in Riverside County, California, that lies about two and a half hours away from Lennox. He had been tortured and suffocated. Kearney remained unknown to law enforcement.

On April 6, 1977, eight-year-old Merle Chance was riding his bike in Kearney's neighborhood near Venice, California. Merle's fifteen-year-old sister watched as he pedaled away from their home and down an alley—the last vision she would have of her brother alive.

Kearney later confessed to seeing Merle on his bike soon after. He stopped the car and leaned over, quickly charming Merle into the passenger seat with the promise of a trip to an amusement park. But soon, Kearney began to panic. What would Merle say to his mother if he ever left the truck alive? Would she call the police? Kearney quickly pulled over. Merle turned and asked meekly, "Are you taking me home now?"

Seven weeks later, a hiker was traversing a trail in Angeles National Forest near Hidden Springs, about an hour's drive from Merle's house. The rainclouds had parted, but droplets still lingered on leaves when the hiker set out on May 26. It would not be long before he came across Merle's shallow grave, marked with rocks left by Kearney. The rain had uncovered the eight-year-old's remains. He had been smothered shortly after his abduction, then brought to Kearney's home before his burial in the forest.

HILL AND KEARNEY TENTATIVELY reunited, but that did not mean his murder series ended. The two still had vicious fights, and Kearney's routine of driving off into the night continued. He prowled the streets outside gay bars, in search of sex workers or someone in need of a ride. He knew he wasn't the only one. Kearney had read about the bodies of gay men strewn along the same roads he drove so often; there was someone else on the prowl as well.

Kearney was not competitive with the man he called the "Wooden Stake," still unknown as Randy Kraft at the time. He didn't need to be—he had no desire to be anything like the Wooden Stake and found any connection later drawn between the two to be offensive. When the law caught up with

Kearney, years before it did with Kraft, police questioned him about the other cases. Kearney had heard of them, had gossiped at the gay bars with other patrons about the murders, but said he had no idea who the Wooden Stake was. When detectives inquired about a possible association between the two, Kearney replied with an annoyed "no."

What about someone other than the Wooden Stake who was involved with murders? Did he know anyone? Kearney told police, "Inadvertently. I lived in Long Island Beach and I did a lot of corresponding with people who put ads in the *Free Press* [a local underground newspaper]." Kearney didn't elaborate, and the identity of his pen pal remains unknown.

Kearney prided himself on the refinement of his murder process. He had gotten it down to a gruesome routine: show a friendly face to a stranger, get him in the car, shoot the unsuspecting passenger with his right hand, guide his Volkswagen bug to a spot hidden from view with his left, perform postmortem sex acts, and dump the body. His last murder, that of seventeen-year-old John LaMay, didn't follow this sequence of events. LaMay would be his undoing.

Sometime in early 1977, LaMay met David Hill at Midtowne Spa, a bathhouse in Los Angeles, and the two hit it off. LaMay had not fully come out of the closet yet and was still downplaying his sexuality to his family. On March 13, 1977, he headed out from his house in El Segundo to visit Hill at his Redondo Beach home. A few days later, his frantic mother called the police. He never came home.

At first, El Segundo officers thought LaMay simply ran away, even though his family protested—that just wasn't in his nature. The police department's attitude remained the same until five days later, on March 18, when LaMay's body was found in Corona near Temescal Canyon. He had been neatly cut up and separated into five trash bags—just as some of the other bodies found throughout Los Angeles—before being placed in an oil drum. LaMay was identified by a description of a birthmark his mother provided to law enforcement; his head and hands had been removed. Police took a closer look at the brands of the duct tape and transparent plastic sealed around LaMay's body and found a clue. The trash bags were industrial, labeled "Mipro 6160" and not commonly available to consumers. A thorough exam of the body also yielded green fibers and unidentified pubic hairs.

Before LaMay drove to Hill and Kearney's home, he told a neighbor he was going to see "Dave," a guy he met at a gym, in Redondo Beach. When LaMay showed up dead, the neighbor ran over the conversation in his head. When he relayed the information to the police, their ears perked up. They had just seen a Dave in the sign-in books at the Midtowne Spa as part of a murder investigation—only it wasn't LaMay's.

Arturo Ramos Marquez was a twenty-four-year-old man from Oxnard who was last seen leaving for dinner with a closeted lawyer he was dating. When Marquez's body was found on March 3, 1977, the lawyer became police's prime suspect. Then LaMay's remains showed up, and the "David Hill" listed on the Midtowne Spa's sign-in sheet lit up in their minds.

RIVERSIDE COUNTY SHERIFF'S DEPUTIES Larry Miller and Dan Wilson showed up to Hill's house unaware they were about to cross the threshold of a homicide scene. It didn't take long to figure it out. Hill and Kearney were both home—and invited Miller and Wilson inside. Immediately, both noticed the green carpet and remembered the fibers left on the duct tape around LaMay's body. While Kearney and Hill shuffled about to make themselves "presentable," the deputies discreetly snagged a sample.

When Miller and Wilson began to question the pair about local murders of gay men, both Hill and Kearney metaphorically clutched their pearls. They were both gay, Kearney pointed out multiple times—they were afraid of killers in the night as well. Besides, Hill had not been home when LaMay was supposedly coming to visit but rather at a friend's house. Kearney had been at work at Hughes Aircraft. Miller and Wilson politely thanked the two for the information and left. They wouldn't be gone for long.

The lab put a rush on the fiber analysis and found a color match. When Miller and Wilson went to the offices of Hughes Aircraft, they found the same brand of trash bags used on LaMay's body lying just feet away from Kearney's desk. Miller and Wilson had enough circumstantial evidence to justify a return to Hill and Kearney's Redondo Beach home, but they needed more for a warrant. Not only would the carpet fibers fail to hold up in court, but they could also dismantle the prosecution's entire case—Miller and Wilson obtained them before they were granted a search warrant. Dubbed "fruit of the poisonous tree" by lawyers, illegally obtained evidence such as the fibers would discount any evidence stemming from their discovery (most notably the trash bags), blocking its entry into a court of law. If they wanted the fibers on the record, Miller and Wilson would have to ask.

For baffling reasons, Hill and Kearney obliged. What about samples of their pubic hair, deputies asked? Fine by them. This was years before DNA was ever used in a criminal case, but microscopic slides of Kearney's samples

P W KEARNEY

ACCUSED—Patrick Kearney, right, on way to
county jail here after new charges were filed.
Times photo by Rick Meyer

Top: Mug shot of Patrick Kearney,
LA Times, June 30, 1977.

Bottom: *LA Times*, February 16, 1978.

and those found on LaMay's body seemed to perfectly align. The search warrant was prepared.

Whatever happened behind closed doors between Hill and Kearney during the LaMay investigation is unclear, but after Miller and Wilson collected the carpet fibers and pubic hair, the couple decided it was time to leave. Before the deputies could return to their home for a third time, now armed with a warrant, the pair headed to El Paso, Texas. Both of their cars were abandoned near the Los Angeles International Airport, leaving law enforcement to wonder whether they had made it to Mexico before they could be captured.

While Kearney and Hill went on the run, Miller and Wilson went to work searching their home. It was all there. Ample traces of blood, a hacksaw with a fresh blade but human remains still jammed in its handle, rubber gloves. Bulletins were sent across California with Kearney's and Hill's photographs beneath the word "WANTED."

On July 1, 1977, Kearney and Hill drove to the Riverside County Sheriff's Office and turned themselves in. While Hill was investigated for a time for possible involvement in Kearney's homicides, no charges were ever filed against him. Either Kearney cleaned up after himself exceptionally well, or Hill lied. Kearney stressed that Hill was innocent—and, just as resolutely, that he himself was not.

Over the following days, Kearney walked law enforcement through his list of victims scattered throughout multiple jurisdictions, not always remembering where their bodies lay. Some have never been found.

Kearney pleaded guilty to twenty-one counts of murder and, as a result of the plea deal, received twenty-one life sentences instead of the death penalty. He is eighty-three years old as of 2022 and will spend his remaining days at Mule Creek State Prison in California.

Chapter 19

DEADLY ALLIANCES

Williated George Bonin murdered at least twenty-one boys and young men between 1979 and 1980 alone. He was later referred to in court as "the most arch-evil person in the world" for his horrific crimes; his victims' wounds shared many similarities with the torture and mutilation of those killed by Kraft. When the discovery of the bodies of Bonin's victims began to make headlines, Kraft realized he was not the only shark in the water.

Despite his apparent attraction to men, Bonin was freshly graduated from high school and engaged to be married to a woman. The two later had a son but divorced shortly thereafter. By then, Bonin had already spent nearly a decade accumulating victims of his physical and sexual abuse. In 1968, at the age of twenty-one, Bonin was first convicted of these heinous crimes.

Prior to his first appearance in court, Bonin served in the United States Air Force and spent five months in Vietnam. He was presented with a medal after going into the direct line of fire in order to save a fellow serviceman. And yet, during the Tet Offensive, he later admitted, he had held two officers at gunpoint and raped them. These atrocities proved to foreshadow a dark practice Bonin came to inflict—one that made his previous crimes pale in comparison.

After Bonin's first convictions, he was sent to Atascadero State Hospital as a patient in need of psychological treatment. It was here where doctors discovered his IQ of 121. He also had notable damage to his prefrontal cortex, an essential component of the brain responsible for a patient's ability to control decisions.

Bonin was later sent to prison after doctors felt they had exhausted all possible treatment options. In 1974, he was released, but three months later, he again perpetrated the same offense—sexual assault—on a fourteen-year-old victim. Again, he went to prison. Despite a maximum sentence of fifteen years, he served less time than his first stint and was released in 1978. He then moved one mile away from his mother's home.

Back in Downey, Bonin befriended a number of boys and young men by providing them with alcohol and a place to party. He got a girlfriend he would take to Anaheim to roller skate. It was during this time Bonin met neighbor Everett Fraser, a forty-three-year-old who often hosted these inappropriate gatherings with teenagers. At these parties, Bonin bonded with twenty-one-year-old Vernon Butts and eighteen-year-old Gregory Miley. The two men went on to join Bonin in several cases of torture and murder.

Bonin's victims were between the ages of twelve and nineteen. Some were still in grade school; others were sex workers or hitchhikers picked up along the road or near gay bars. Their unspeakable deaths were precluded by some of the worst torture known to those who study serial killers. Beatings, stabbings, mutilation, and strangulation were among Bonin's signatures; several bodies were linked through the presence of an ice pick protruding from one ear. One victim was tortured to such a degree, he died of shock before Bonin could administer his final blow. Most were killed in Bonin's van and then left near freeways in Southern California.

Bonin was again arrested in 1979—not for murder, but for molestation of a minor. Before he could even settle into his cell, an administrative error caused his release; this mistake proved fatal to over a dozen subsequent victims. Astoundingly, this would not be the only catastrophic failure of law enforcement to prevent even more murders.

On February 4, 1980, Bonin was arrested for violating his parole and remained in jail until one month later. Ten days following his release, Bonin killed again. One of his survivors provided the key to his final capture. This survivor, however, was no innocent.

In March 1980, seventeen-year-old William Pugh was abducted by Bonin. In a hideously mystifying turn of events, after Pugh was spared from abuse or death, he joined Bonin in the subsequent murder of fifteen-year-old runaway Harry Todd Turner, bludgeoning him before Bonin strangled him to death.

When Pugh was arrested for auto theft the following May, he learned of a $50,000 reward for the so-called Freeway Killer, who was, in fact, Bonin (Randy Kraft and Patrick Kearney also shared this moniker due to some of their victim dump sites). Pugh went to his counselor with his "suspicions," failing to mention his own participation in Turner's murder. When police looked into Bonin, they found his rap sheet, and they began to surveille his movements on June 2, 1980.

The very same day, Bonin began a hunt for a new victim—this time with a different accomplice, James Munro. The two met after Bonin came across a homeless Munro and struck up a friendship with him. Bonin eventually invited Munro to move in. At this point, Bonin and his mother, Alice, were living together. Bonin and Munro began a sexual relationship, which somehow not only remained intact but flourished when Bonin revealed he wanted the two of them to commit murder together.

Hours after surveillance began on June 2, Bonin and Munro lured eighteen-year-old Steven Jay Wells into Bonin's van and strangled him to death. They packed Wells's body in a cardboard box and drove it to the home of Vernon Butts, one of the men Bonin met at Everett Fraser's apartment. Butts participated in at least eight of Bonin's murders—one victim was a seventeen-year-old, the boy who died of shock during extreme torture.

When Bonin and Munro revealed Wells's body to Butts, he exclaimed, "Oh, you got another one!" and then advised the two on where to dump the body. Bonin thought a nearby canyon was best but wound up following Butts's lead, leaving Wells behind a Huntington Beach gas station, where he was found just five hours later.

Bonin was supposedly under surveillance at the time of the Watts murder; how had this gone unnoticed by police? Eight days passed before Bonin was arrested—but not for Watts's death. Rather, Bonin was observed trolling around Hollywood in search of victims. After five attempts to lure different teenage boys into his van for a hookup, Bonin finally succeeded with seventeen-year-old Harold Eugene Tate. Tate entered Bonin's van, but police did not yet intervene. Instead of immediately pulling Bonin over, they followed him until he parked in an empty lot close to the freeway, where they slowly approached the van. After screams and banging were heard, police finally entered the vehicle, where they found Bonin raping a handcuffed Tate. The hesitance—the inaction—of law enforcement to prevent this assault is unthinkable.

After his arrest, Bonin's van was searched and found to be full of evidence, including various apparatus used in the murders, alongside a stomach-churning amount of dried blood. Despite a confession, Bonin pleaded not guilty during his trial.

Bonin's lawyers mounted a defense centered on his horrific childhood. The elements of Bonin's youth are inarguably unimaginable to most people—his early years are full of what many consider to be the foundation of a serial killer's development.

Born on January 8, 1947, Bonin was the second of three sons of Robert and Alice Bonin. Robert and Alice were both alcoholics, and the family became permeated with neglect, physical abuse, and deprivation of the children's basic necessities. Food and clothing were regularly provided to Bonin and his brothers not by their parents but by neighbors who could not turn a blind eye to children in need. But even these experiences would pale in comparison to what befell Bonin throughout his early years.

Alice's father routinely served as her sons' caretaker. It was under his watch that Bonin began to experience sexual molestation, with his own grandfather as the perpetrator. Alice's father was well experienced in these crimes; he had abused Alice as a child as well. She knew. And yet, again and again, she brought her sons into the clutches of her abuser.

When Bonin was six years old, his mother sent him to an orphanage as an escape from his father, whose extreme beatings regularly put the children's lives at risk. It was at this institution that Bonin suffered abuse so severe, it is the only period of his life he never shared with anyone, aside from acknowledging to psychologists that several authority figures had sexually abused him. He was six to nine years old at the time.

After three years at the orphanage, Bonin returned to his family and soon began to establish his criminal record. Sent to juvenile hall at the age of ten for stealing license plates, Bonin was, once again, sexually abused, this time by adults at the institution, including his own youth counselor. Following his release, his family relocated to California, where his father died shortly thereafter from cirrhosis. It was there, in the city of Downey, that Bonin began to inflict the same horrendous abuse he had suffered on others. Even his brothers wouldn't be spared.

Despite the argument against his guilt based on his childhood, Bonin ultimately received multiple death sentences. During the fourteen years he spent in prison prior to his death by lethal injection on February 23, 1996, Bonin focused much of his time on creative projects, such as poetry and art. He also grew fond of cards and began playing with a few fellow inmates. One of his favorite bridge partners was Randy Steven Kraft.

William Bonin. *Courtesy of Wikimedia Commons.*

Chapter 20

COMPARE TO CONTRAST

comparison of Kraft, Kearney, and Bonin versus the Doodler yields a mixed bag of results. The brightest of red flags waves from the lack of evidence of sexual activity in any of the Doodler victims' autopsies. Kraft, Kearney, and Bonin had all expressed in no uncertain terms that their murders were sexually motivated; the Doodler case, however, is less clear-cut.

As Dr. Allan Branson noted, absence of sexual activity in no way rules out a sexual motivation for a murder. The use of a knife as a symbolic phallus, or piquerism, is a known phenomenon. Still, the crime scenes of the Doodler versus those of Kraft, Kearney, and Bonin differ in several other major ways.

The Doodler is the only killer of the four who did not dump his victims. Gerald, Jae, Klaus, Frederick, and Harald were all found in the same location where they were attacked. Apart from dragging one victim approximately twenty feet so he would not lie sprawled directly across a hiking path, the Doodler made no effort to majorly delay the discovery of any of the bodies. That did not mean he was the only one showing off, though; Kraft and Bonin both earned the nickname "the Freeway Killer" due to the sprawled bodies they left out in the open for drivers to spot, often shortly after the victims' deaths. Kearney, though he left some bodies by the roadside, often dumped corpses at landfills, in canyons, or in desert areas, where they were quickly scavenged by local wildlife.

The Doodler's known hunting grounds within the gay nightlife scene are an aspect of his case he shares with all three other serial killers. Survivors of the Doodler tell of his charming personality, just as the friends and families of Kraft and Kearney did. Forty-four people thought well enough of Randy Kraft that they testified in his defense at his sentencing hearing.

Kraft, Kearney, and Bonin all additionally picked up hitchhikers. It is unknown whether the Doodler ever did—or whether he posed as a hitchhiker himself. Jae Stevens possibly drove the Doodler to Spreckels Lake, where he was murdered. It is unclear whether any of the other Doodler victims' cars were located near the murder locations.

William Bonin had confirmed accomplices. Kraft claims his own innocence to this day and, therefore, maintains there were no accomplices to be had. Kearney never strayed from his confession that he killed completely alone. However, there was significant evidence in Kraft and Kearney's cases, both circumstantial and physical, that an unidentified person or persons assisted in several murders. Conversely, the San Francisco Police Department has maintained for decades that the Doodler Murders were the act of one killer.

Kraft, Kearney, and Bonin all served in the armed forces at one point. Did the Doodler's Navy watch cap mean anything, or was it simply a stylistic choice? Was he genuinely a commercial art student, or was he a member of the military? Aside from the Navy watch cap, there is no public evidence as to whether there is a connection between the Doodler and the armed forces.

Until the identity of the Doodler is finally revealed, the only certainty is that he, Kraft, Kearney, and Bonin all preyed on gay men in California during the 1970s (with all but the Doodler confirmed to have killed more widely as well). All four robbed a total of over 130 men and boys of their lives, some whose families were left utterly devastated beyond repair and others whose families, to this day, are still unaware of their deaths, forever wondering whatever became of their loved one.

Chapter 21

ALL OVER AGAIN

In San Francisco, the Doodler case was falling apart brick by brick. The surviving witnesses would not come forward. Dr. Priest's testimony could not be admitted in court. The San Francisco Police Department had linked no physical evidence to a person of interest. No witnesses had officially placed the man Gilford and Sanders suspected at the scene of the murders. The mountain they had climbed to reach the conclusion of these investigations began to collapse in on itself. Though Gilford and Sanders were confident the victims were murdered by a man who impressed them with his artwork, no drawings were ever recovered. Even worse, gay men started to go missing from the Castro again. Then came the phone calls. More bodies had been found.

Tunitas Creek Road lies south of San Francisco, just inland from Half Moon Bay. Its pavement weaves through the Santa Cruz Mountains along steep slopes that flatten to form Tunitas Creek. The road's beauty has made it a top choice for California cyclists—at least those who can handle the incline. It was here, under the canopy of ancient trees, where a serial killer would dump the bodies of his victims.

The start of April 1978 was still too chilly to feel like spring, the high temperature barely crossing over into the fifties. Still, the new season was just around the corner. A local real estate agent brought a client to a home on Tunitas Creek Road, hoping to nudge the man's interest into a sale.

Tunitas Creek Road. *Photo by Matty Dowlen. Courtesy of the artist.*

When the agent brought the client to a high point overlooking the available property, all serenity shattered. Lying below them, alongside the road, was the body of twenty-seven-year-old Ronald Young.

Two weeks earlier, on the other side of the ridgeline, twenty-four-year-old Daniel Joseph Oller's body was also found in a picturesque stretch of the mountains near Huddard Park. A woman had taken her horse for a morning walk when she spotted Oller, halfway naked and clearly deceased. Young's murder signaled that Oller's demise might not have been a singular incident. It was later apparent that neither was.

Oller was from Redwood City, where he attended Sequoia High School. After his teenage years, he became a sex worker and frequented the streets of San Francisco. Young shared this occupation but was, instead, from Texas. He made his way west in search of a new beginning. There, he met his end.

On June 7, just over two months after Ronald Young's body was discovered, police returned to Tunitas Creek Road to find not one but two bodies lying a few hundred yards away from where the real estate agent had spotted Young's corpse. Identifying the pair would prove to be a challenge that rivaled the investigation of the case itself; the bodies were in such a decomposed state, obtaining fingerprints was its own struggle. It is unclear when one of the victims was identified as Raymond Oscar Wilson; as of 2022, any information related to his death is sealed by the San Mateo County coroner's office. Other than confirmation of his name, San Mateo would provide no additional information about Wilson's age or birthplace. He was found alongside the man still known as John Doe #78-2.

Both Wilson and Doe were found wearing only blue jeans—just as Oller and Young had been. All of the men were tied up prior to their murders, with the restraints removed before their bodies were disposed of and the killer slipped back into the night. All had bruises around the stomach and groin regions. All were strangled with ligatures.

Months passed with no breaks in the case. Before any would come, another body was found. Police returned to Tunitas Creek Road on October 6, after Arthur Tomlin Goodman III's body was discovered. Originally from New York, Goodman had no formal employment at the time of his murder. He spent the last night of his life socializing at a bar in the Tenderloin. The next morning, police found his body, clothed in a striped polo shirt and jeans, stuffed into a sleeping bag. Despite the minor differences in Goodman's case (he was fully clothed, and his body was concealed), police later confirmed they had linked his murder to those of Oller, Young, Wilson, and Doe. Someone had turned Tunitas Creek Road into a graveyard.

The killer's methods seemed strikingly familiar. He met with men in San Francisco and charmed them into joining him on a dark and remote stretch of scenic Northern California, where they would meet their end. This time, the investigation involved two separate jurisdictions: the San Mateo County Sheriff's Office and the SFPD. While the bodies were found near Half Moon Bay, the victims had been traced back to the city of San Francisco, and the locations of the actual murders remained unknown.

This time, there was a greater show of law enforcement than the Doodler's case had received in its beginning stages. The SFPD was now no stranger to murders within the gay community, and they wanted the public to know these crimes were being actively investigated.

Chapter 22

SWEET SORROW

Rotea Gilford's achievements in the San Francisco Police Department had not gone unnoticed by then-mayor George Moscone. In May 1978, the fifteen commendations Gilford received over his eighteen-year career at the SFPD landed him an appointment by Moscone as executive director of the Mayor's Council on Criminal Justice. Roughly a month after the first body was found in San Mateo, Gilford reported for his first day on the job. When Stephen Hall of the *San Francisco Chronicle* interviewed him following the announcement, Gilford struck a somber tone as he spoke of his departure from the homicide unit:

> *Catching killers is a very saddening thing. You see a very dismal side of reality. After a while, you begin to feel the world is full of some pretty crummy people. You have to say to yourself, "Hey, that's really not what the world is like."…And I'm not going to miss the tears, the heartache of the bereaved that always follows the homicides. One tragedy after another.*

At the same time, leaving the SFPD and his partner, Earl Sanders, without solving the Doodler Murders was not an easy choice: "I'm going to miss the excitement. I am leaving some of the most challenging cases I've had in my career."

In his new role on the mayor's council, Gilford's workload shifted from bloody crime scenes to creating innovative program proposals for criminal justice reform in San Francisco. "The aim is to cut the rate of recidivism, reduce the rate of crime, and assist the police department," he said. Some set their sights on other ambitions for Gilford. Willie Brown (then a Democratic assemblyman in San Francisco) thought he should become the county sheriff, but Moscone's offer appealed more to Gilford, as it provided a better path toward his ultimate goal: to combat the institutional racism deeply embedded throughout the criminal justice system. "At least I'll have a better opportunity to make my views known, to be heard, and to hear first-hand how those department heads intend to make the changes that are necessary in San Francisco," he told the *Chronicle*.

Homicide detective Rotea Gilford. *Courtesy of the SFPD.*

This next step in Gilford's journey was earned the hard way—through thousands of hours of grinding police work that bled over into his family home; the massive amount of time he spent away from his wife, Judi, often strained their marriage, nearly to the breaking point. They were married in 1974, a year after he and his first wife, Patricia, divorced—Gilford's workload had played a starring role in the breakdown of the relationship.

Many a night had been spent oscillating between deep conversation and lighthearted card games with Earl Sanders, who never failed to provide Gilford with a shoulder when needed. In the summer of 1977, Gilford quietly suffered the worst pain a parent can imagine when his son, Michael, spent months slowly deteriorating from a severe internal infection. On October 11, 1977, the mysterious illness proved fatal. Michael attended the U.S. Naval Academy in Annapolis, Maryland, and shared his father's passion for football there, playing for both the Naval Academy and Santa Clara University after he transferred. The months between his infection and his death were filled with a wide range of failed treatments; multiple surgeries and massive doses of antibiotics could not save Michael from his end. Gilford had tried everything—even working with the Center for Disease Control to find a cure. There was no closure after Michael passed away, for when his autopsy was given to the family, no explanation for the infection could be found. Gilford never got over it—as experienced by any parent who has lost a child. It was very likely that this pain, this loss, played a role in Gilford stepping away from the homicide unit and into the mayor's office. His partner and dear friend, Earl Sanders, understood.

Dubbed the "Soul Brothers" by their fellow officers, Gilford and Sanders parted ways and ended an era. The SFPD and San Mateo County teamed up in search of the man responsible for the bodies found near Tunitas Creek sans Gilford. While he moved on to the mayor's office and away from the Doodler investigation, the San Mateo murders picked up where the Doodler killings left off.

Chapter 23

ICARUS OF THE GOLDEN CITY

I n 1978, Detective Dave Toschi spoke to reporters several times regarding the wave of violent killings in the gay community. The four-year-old Doodler Murders investigation had not reached a conclusion, and the grisly San Mateo murders presented a fresh opportunity for the SFPD to get a killer into handcuffs. When the Doodler case began to heat up in its earlier stages, Toschi made sure to alert the press of his ties to the investigation. His penchant for reporters, however, had been wearing on some San Franciscans for years.

Ever since the Zodiac case began in 1969, Toschi had embedded himself as a consistently featured name in San Francisco publications—so much so that famed writer Armistead Maupin included him as a character in his *Tales of the City* column in the *San Francisco Chronicle*. In it, Toschi played the role of investigator in the fictional search for the "Tinkerbell" killer, a supposedly gay man who strangled his victims and left them covered in glitter. As it turned out, the real killer in Maupin's fictional series was one of Toschi's fellow officers, who attempted to frame a local trans woman for the murders. While the series had no shortage of public criticism, the bottom line was that it became one of the most popular sections of the *Chronicle*, blurring the lines between the newspaper's presentation of fact and fiction.

Maupin proved to be Toschi's undoing. When a letter signed with the Zodiac symbol showed up in the *Chronicle*'s mailbox in April 1978, he went public with a secret he had kept for two years. Maupin alleged that Toschi had previously written him self-congratulatory letters and signed them with fictitious names. When the 1978 Zodiac letter was received after a four-year gap in communication from the killer, Maupin's red flags went up. He believed Toschi himself had written the Zodiac note and mailed it to the *Chronicle*, just as he had his letters to Maupin.

The result was scrutiny of nearly every Zodiac letter—could Toschi have written them all? An internal investigation began. On July 11, 1978—Toschi's forty-seventh birthday—he reported to the SFPD not as a member of the homicide unit but for his new assignment in the pawnshop detail. The backlash from both Toschi's supporters and detractors sent a wave throughout the city.

Those who felt Toschi's need for praise was a weakness but not a mortal sin denied his authorship of the Zodiac letter, while acknowledging the letters to Maupin and the *Chronicle* sent under a pseudonym were genuine. On July 23, 1978, Guy Wright wrote a piece in the *San Francisco Examiner* titled "A Fan Letter for Dave Toschi." In it, Wright listed a number of Toschi's unpublicized accomplishments in the SFPD homicide unit—such as saving a suicidal woman from jumping off a cliff and into the surf at Ocean Beach, as well as making a $1,000 donation to a murder victim's family. "They say he loved publicity. Many people do. But the times he came to me for publicity, it was because he cared for someone else."

Toschi portrayed as a martyr didn't sit well with many San Franciscans. Within the gay community, his fall from grace was confirmation of what some had always thought—Toschi was disingenuous at best. San Francisco's two main LGBTQ newspapers, the *San Francisco Sentinel* and the *Bay Area Reporter*, went to battle over his guilt. Years prior, the *Reporter* had published a piece on numerous unsolved murders of gay men and the failures of the SFPD to catch the killers. The *Sentinel* published a rebuke of the article, implying that Toschi was one of the gay community's strongest allies and besmirching his reputation didn't help murder victims. When Toschi was investigated in 1978, Paul-Francis Hartmann of the *Reporter* referenced the *Sentinel* piece, writing sarcastically, "Gay murders were Toschi's private preserve—he was working hard—he was above criticism—what more could anyone ask?" When it came to Toschi's demotion and the subsequent onslaught of negative press, Hartmann spared no ounce of venomous condemnation:

> *Deep-sixing over the Golden Gate railing must surely have crossed Toschi's mind these last weeks. And perhaps he finally grasps in one bright flash what went through the minds of all those gay murder victims he so glibly handled. In the throes of being DESTROYED, one succumbs to the horror....Why*

fight it.…Isn't that what they always wanted? Think of all those troubled
spirits who now have a justice of sorts. Now he knows what it's like.

By the time bodies from the Castro started showing up in San Mateo County, Toschi's public profile had plummeted to the depths of utmost contempt.

THE AUTHENTICITY OF THE 1978 Zodiac letter Toschi was accused of writing remains a debate among investigators. What is certain is his reputation as a public official hungry for the spotlight did nothing to encourage the gay community's faith in the SFPD. By the time the San Mateo murders gained the public's attention in October 1978, Toschi had been demoted for months. Gilford and Sanders's investigation of the Doodler had stalled out, with no evidence to arrest anyone in the case.

Just as Gay Action and the Butterfly Brigade had, the LGBTQ community stepped in to try to nudge forward the investigation of the San Mateo murders. The Tavern Guild offered a reward for information on the killer, just as they had with the Doodler. An October 1978 article in the *San Francisco Examiner* noted how the San Mateo murders stirred the memory of the still-unsolved Doodler case. Even so, the threat of a serial killer paled in comparison to the homophobic violence that was plaguing the gay community. Journalist Bill Boldenweck wrote,

> *Attacks on gays of all appearances are frequent, and some would-be attacks*
> *on gays hit straight people who only seem gay to the assailants, people in the*
> *gay community say. So there is a constant edge of fear in the bars along Polk*
> *and Castro and Folsom Streets, and in the Victorian flats in the inner Mission*
> *and on Russian Hill. But there isn't yet a specific fear about the five men who*
> *were strangled and dumped in San Mateo County near the coast.*

Wayne Friday, then-president of the Tavern Guild, told Boldenweck the case of the San Mateo murders wasn't being ignored. As he put it, "We're prepared to offer a substantial reward in this case if it turns out to be another case where someone is preying on members of the gay community here. But at this point, I don't think anyone in the community has thought of these cases in that light." That quickly changed.

Less than two weeks after Boldenweck's *Examiner* piece ran, the *Bay Area Reporter* detailed the San Mateo murders, alerting the gay community that a killer walked among them once again.

Chapter 24

A NEW PREDATOR STALKS THE CASTRO

At that point, the SFPD teamed up with the San Mateo County Sherriff's Office in search for the killer who had been luring gay men to be murdered near Tunitas Creek. After the discovery of Tom Goodman's body in October 1978, law enforcement strongly felt his murder had been committed by the same man who killed Daniel Oller, Ronald Young, Raymond Oscar Wilson, and the still-unidentified John Doe #78-2.

It wasn't only the bodies' locations and the use of strangulation that pointed law enforcement toward this conclusion. There were other potentially major clues. Four of the five victims were found wearing only blue jeans. Goodman had also been wearing jeans but was found with a striped polo shirt in addition. All of them had been restrained prior to their deaths, as seen by ligature marks on their wrists and ankles. In all cases, these restraints had been removed prior to the dumping of the bodies. Police told the press that most of the victims had been struck; the San Mateo County Sherriff's Office would not release any of the autopsies as of 2022, but dental records of John Doe #78-2 show seven of his teeth had broken off. In Goodman's case, police would only comment that there was "evidence of sexual activity" but provided no further details, and the question of whether this evidence exists in the other cases went unanswered. All of the victims were tied to San Francisco's gay community, as well as what police called "narcotics activities." The *Bay Area Reporter* described the victims as "Castro

Clones"—a term used to describe white, gay men with short, neatly trimmed hair, who wore jeans and were clean-shaven except for a tidy mustache.

Though similarities existed between the five victims, law enforcement did not have enough information to allow a zeroed-in search of the murderer's location. Without assistance from the public, the investigation began to stall out, just as the Doodler case had. Once again, the police turned to the press—the individual murders had barely received any coverage up to that point, but the threat of another serial killer preying on San Francisco's gay community turned out to be a more enticing story to reporters.

A few days after the *San Francisco Examiner* ran a story on the case, journalist Bill Boldenweck wrote an article on the October 16, 1978 discovery of another body along Tunitas Creek, a few miles from where the known victims were found. The corpse had not been identified. Police told Boldenweck that despite the body's location, there was not enough evidence to tie this victim to the others.

The man was made to kneel before he was shot in the back of the neck, execution-style. He died instantly, and his body then tumbled down a one-hundred-foot slope to the edge of Tunitas Creek. Boldenweck's *Examiner* article included a description of his body; it was apparent he was a Navy sailor, as evidenced by numerous tattoos. Among them were the words "Little Rock CLG 4," the name "Nancy," an eagle, a star, and a pair of roses. Two weeks later, word reached Dubuque, Iowa, and John Doe was identified as Thomas Woodward, a thirty-seven-year-old silversmith. Woodward had moved to Port Costa, about an hour-and-a-half drive to Tunitas Creek Road, just eleven days prior to his murder. Police told the *Contra Costa Times* they theorized Woodward had been the victim of a robbery, as he possibly had valuable jewelry with him at the time. This was linked to his profession, and no further evidence was presented by police to back up the theory. As of 2022, Woodward's case remains unsolved. Less than six weeks after his body was found, San Mateo law enforcement felt even more confident Woodward's murder was unrelated to the other victims.

Chapter 25

THE NICE GUY

A lot of people liked David Likens. People were drawn to his smile, warmth, and generosity. Even prison guards at San Quentin would come to agree. Likens, at thirty-one, had walked a fairly winding road through life so far. Born on July 12, 1947, in Arizona, he began his Army service on July 26, 1966, but his tour of duty was cut short after less than a year for unknown reasons. After moving to Hollywood, Likens worked his way up to a field coordinator position at a construction firm but soon found bartending better suited his lifestyle.

Likens shone in the nightlife scene, and his lean physique and sandy blond hair drew no shortage of suitors. His charm and conversational finesse soon made him a favorite of numerous patrons at the bar. When it came to his inner circle, one member later testified to Likens's personality: "He was a likeable, popular person who would do anything to help a friend—and he had plenty of friends." There was one exception to Likens's otherwise cheerful demeanor; the same friend said that when Likens was drunk, he "allegedly became a Dr. Jekyll/Mr. Hyde person." Another friend later told press,

> *His alcoholism was his biggest problem. He had to escape from reality. He sought and received acceptance from others, but he was very unhappy. He went to LA for a couple of years to escape his problems—including his problems with sado-masochism. Dave was a helluva [sic] nice guy when he wasn't drinking. He was "butch" and well-built—6 [feet tall], blonde,*

*blue eyes. Dave was always helping people—moving them and painting for
friends and loaning everyone money when he had it.*

Likens had indeed gone to Los Angeles to try to change his future. Instead,
he ended the life of Ronald "Rod" Eugene Tharp, a young hitchhiker and
possible sex worker. Very little is known of Tharp's case, but the details
that did make it to the press turned the stomachs of many a reader. Likens
probably picked up Tharp while cruising the gay bars of Los Angeles. Once
he lured Tharp back to his apartment, Likens killed him—but it is unclear
how. What is known is when Tharp's body was wheeled out of Likens's
apartment bound for the medical examiner, it bore scratches on the chest
and abdomen, stab wounds, and marks of strangulation. Tharp was found
in Likens's bathtub. His genitals had also been mutilated.

The details of the investigation are still tightly sealed by the Los Angeles
Police Department—as of 2022, not even Tharp's coroner's report has
been released to the public. Likens's arrest on April 12, 1974, however, is on
record. He was picked up on the same day he murdered Rod Tharp.

At first, Likens pleaded not guilty to second-degree homicide charges.
The district attorney's office began to prepare for trial. When Likens
entered the courtroom on December 3, 1974, something had changed.
Likens walked in alongside his representation, named in court records
as S.P. Berg, H. Vites, and G. Taylor. The defense had filed a motion to
dismiss evidence gathered at Likens's home and on his person as fruit of
the poisonous tree. There was no search warrant; therefore, any and all
evidence pointing to his guilt stemming from that illegal search should be
inadmissible in court.

Both the prosecution and the judge, however, thought differently. Jay
A. Lipton, the deputy district attorney who represented the people of Los
Angeles County, stood to provide his objection grounds to the court. Lipton
either misspoke or was misquoted when he cited the Fourteenth Amendment
to the United States Constitution (which provided citizenship and equal civil
and legal rights to Black Americans and enslaved peoples who had been
emancipated after the Civil War) instead of the Fourth Amendment, which
relates to search and seizures by the government.

Of particular interest was the case of *People vs. Wallace* in 1973. On March
1 of the same year, Henry Wallace called police to his home for assistance
with his injured wife. When law enforcement showed up and found a
stabbed Mrs. Wallace, her husband voluntarily accompanied police down
to the station for questioning. While he remained there, a police evidence

technician arrived at the Wallace home and discovered a bloody knife in a drawer—without a warrant. When defense counsel attempted to block the knife and all other evidence gathered at the house in trial, the Supreme Court of Contra Costa County denied the motion. Judge Robert H. London of the Superior Court of Los Angeles did the same, after lengthy presentations by both counsel in chambers. Likens and his lawyers would have to do better than the Wallace case.

Mr. Berg, one of Likens's lawyers, didn't miss a beat. If the motion was denied, Likens wanted to change his plea from not guilty to guilty and waive his right to a jury trial. Judge London wanted to definitively confirm both Likens and his counsel were steadfast in their decision. Judge London stressed that he did not view this as a sentencing deal—the only thing both the court and the prosecution committed to was sending Likens to a correctional counselor for a diagnostic examination and study. The analysis would be conducted by the counselor alongside a psychiatrist; together, they would make a sentencing recommendation to the court—almost always a choice between probation or time at a state prison.

While Judge London did commit to the examination, he made it crystal clear to both Likens and his counsel that he might not agree with the diagnostic assessment, saying "The bottom-line sentencing in this case is discretionary with me, an individual, as a Judge in this case." He turned to address Likens directly and said, "Now the reason for that is very simple. I know nothing about you. Do you understand that, sir?" Likens did. Judge London and the prosecution went on to list the numerous constitutionally protected rights Likens was waiving with his plea of guilty. A variation of the same question was asked seven times: Was Likens making this plea of his own volition, or had he been coerced in any way, shape or form? The repetition was possibly due to Likens's freshly broken nose, still swollen and darkly bruised. If the plea had been forced, Judge London wanted to know about it. Likens responded seven times to confirm that his plea was both true and voluntary.

Likens wanted probation for Tharp's murder, and the defense submitted the motion before the court. Judge London agreed to a hearing to consider—but made it clear to Likens and the defense that regardless of the recommendation provided to him by the Probation Department, he was much more likely to send Likens to the State Department of Corrections for a diagnostic study. The defense had another request: that Likens be treated for the broken nose he received during a jailhouse altercation for reasons unknown. Judge London agreed.

Next up was phone and visitor privileges. Mrs. Buckner, Likens's mother, was entered into the record as present in courtroom. The defense asked when she would be returning to her home in Tucson. She had flown in from Arizona, Likens's birth state, when the news came in of his arrest. No public record exists detailing her interactions with her son after Tharp's murder—did her presence have any effect on Likens's change of plea?

Despite her son admitting to the court that he was, in fact, a murderer, Buckner didn't want to leave him yet. Could she come with Likens's lawyers to visit him before his sentencing? Judge London said no but sympathized, adding, "I would [let you] if I had the power to do so."

LIKENS'S PROBATION REQUEST WAS denied by Judge London, and he entered San Quentin on July 8, 1975. Almost immediately, he accumulated a number of allies. Likens made it clear he was gay, and his openness about his sexual identity gained him respect within the prison. Within months, he was transferred to Sierra Conservation Center, a minimum-security prison near Sonora, California. There, he worked as an office clerk. A correctional officer later remarked, "He had a very good work rapport....There were no disciplinary write-ups. In fact, there were several laudatory comments for good performance."

The same charm Likens used on his victims was also of great use in prison—so much so that on November 8, 1977, barely over two years since he began his sentence, Likens walked out of Sierra Conservation Center a free man. There has been no clear explanation as to why he was released; bewildered law enforcement officials later pointed to the glowing recommendations regularly documented throughout Likens's prison file. The transcript of Likens's original sentencing hearing has been lost to time, but it's possible Judge London chose to adhere to the minimum punishment required by California law: five years in state prison. That sentence would have been greatly reduced if Judge London chose to include Likens's time served, which spanned hundreds of days between numerous hearings and subsequent psychiatric evaluations.

Likens left Sonora and headed to San Francisco.

POLICE THEORIZED THAT LIKENS, like the Doodler, used his flirtatious wit to lure men away from gay bars in San Francisco and into his clutches. He had three known surviving victims who were tied up—just as one of the Doodler's Fox Plaza survivors had been. In Likens's case, at least one of his surviving victims went on the record, and charges were filed. After Likens was apprehended for sexual assault on October 12, 1978, his friend Danny Hepburn got to thinking. Hepburn had seen the news coverage announcing the discovery of Tom Goodman's body along Tunitas Creek Road; suddenly, it clicked.

Goodman was last seen at the Balcony, a gay bar at 2166 Market Street in San Francisco, on October 5, 1978. Three witnesses later told police Goodman was with Likens that night. After Goodman's body was found the following day, an October 26 article in the *Bay Area Reporter* petitioned anyone who had seen him before he died to contact the police. What the public didn't know was the SFPD wasn't looking for a suspect— they were working to confirm that the man they had taken into custody two weeks prior, David Allen Likens, was responsible for the San Mateo murders. Likens was already in jail for felonious assault and attempted murder charges, thanks to information provided from his surviving victims. It was Danny Hepburn who helped add homicide to the list of accusations.

One of Likens's former roommates had seen him and Goodman together the night before the murder. The two had not been alone, the roommate told police; an unidentified third man went off with Likens and Goodman "for sexual activity." Hepburn wasn't there that night; he had left for a vacation on September 30 and let Likens borrow his apartment until he returned on October 9, three days after Goodman's body was found. When Hepburn came home, he couldn't find his leather jacket. Likens provided no explanation but did replace Hepburn's jacket with another, in addition to a portable radio as a thank-you for the accommodations. Both of the items belonged to Tom Goodman. When police picked up Likens shortly thereafter for homicide, he was sporting Goodman's Bulova wristwatch. Police knew they had their man.

Likens's arrest was picked up by news outlets across the country. The year prior, the bloody tale of Patrick Wayne Kearney's decade-long murder series had gotten significant coverage—and while both he and Likens were in custody, Randy Steven Kraft was still free to murder at his leisure. While these killers made far fewer headlines than the Zodiac or Charles Manson, the pattern of gay men winding up dead along California roadsides did not go unnoticed. That Likens had already been found guilty of murdering Rod Tharp in Los Angeles, only to serve barely over two years for the crime, made the story even more shocking to the public—and served as further affirmation that law enforcement simply did not take murders of gay men as seriously as other homicides.

The murder of Thomas Woodward, the thirty-seven-year-old Iowan silversmith found shot execution-style and dumped along Tunitas Creek Road, had not been the work of Likens. Woodward was found on October 16 shortly after his death—four days after Likens was arrested. Woodward's killer remains unidentified.

The pressure for justice for Likens's victims was on Lieutenant Brendan McGuire, who led the coalition of San Francisco and San Mateo County investigators in Likens's arrest. Law enforcement and the district attorney's office prepared to take Likens to trial.

LIKENS NEVER MADE IT to the courtroom. On January 19, 1979, he sat alongside seven other inmates in his cell in the San Mateo County jail. The barred door slid open, and the other men exited to make phone calls or play cards in the recreation room. Likens stayed behind.

At nine-thirty that evening, nurse Pam Ketzler went to Likens's cell to administer an unidentified medication. She, alongside jailer deputy William Buckwalter, found Likens hanging by his bedsheet from the hook of a punching bag. Next to his body lay a note addressed to Tom Nolan, his attorney. It read, in part:

> *I would like to say that I leave with a clear conscience as I did not commit the murders I was charged with. This situation has shown me, however, that I will always be vulnerable to charges every time some kook kills somebody....I have never deliberately hurt anyone and the only person I am (or ever was) capable of killing is (or was) myself....I am not feeling sorry for myself, just too tired to continue in this life without any real goals.*

It wasn't the ending Lieutenant McGuire or anyone else involved in the investigation wanted. McGuire told the press, "It's very disappointing. We put in a lot of work and hours and built up a good case. We're kind of upset he didn't go to trial."

Less than two months after Likens's suicide, more details of his life in San Francisco were uncovered. On March 8, 1979, the SFPD raided a male escort service based in the Mission District, dismantling what was perhaps the largest business of its kind during that period. The sting on the Richard Elmon Escort Service (named after the alias of its owner and operator,

Clifton Lee) resulted in the arrests of fifty-two-year-old Lee, twenty-six-year-old Toby Birch, and nineteen-year-old Paul Clemons. Lee was charged with "pimping and pandering," and Birch and Clemons faced charges of "soliciting an act of prostitution." After police tore through Lee's files, they found a familiar name on his employee roster: David Likens.

It was another, unnamed coworker of Birch and Clemons who had pulled the rug out from under the operation. The man reported Lee to the police and described the business model: Lee charged customers between $45 and $150 for services and kept 40 percent of the fee. Between the ten or so escorts employed by Lee, the business raked in up to $4,000 per week.

When Lee was interviewed at his home, he sported a velour robe and dirty T-shirt—not clothing reflective of the hundreds of thousands of dollars in his possession. When asked about Likens, Lee had a curious response, telling the *San Francisco Examiner*, "I ran a safe and sane operation. I don't have any victims." Did anyone claim he had? It is unclear as to whether Lee was further investigated by the SFPD. The charges of "pimping and pandering," however, convinced a jury to send him to state prison for five years.

The investigation of Likens's alleged murders ground to a halt. As of 2022, the cold case unit of the San Mateo County Sheriff's Office is still unable to identify John Doe #78-2, found dumped near Tunitas Creek Road alongside Raymond Oscar Wilson.

Chapter 26

THE END OF TWO ERAS

Twenty years before the SFPD pulled out the Doodler files for a fresh review, it lost one of its most essential resources in the case. In 1998, at the age of seventy, Rotea Gilford succumbed to a battle with diabetes that had been raging for several years. His left foot, part of his right leg, and a finger were lost in the fight.

There was no shortage of loving tributes from San Franciscans, both on the streets and in the city's highest offices. Then-mayor Willie Brown had been a close friend for decades and stayed by Gilford's side until the very end, visiting his deathbed several hours before his passing. Senator Dianne Feinstein told the *San Francisco Examiner* that Gilford was "leaving a very strong legacy." It was Earl Sanders, by that time the assistant police chief at the SFPD, who made sure that Gilford's efforts to protect the gay community did not go unnoticed.

While Dave Toschi had been positioned as the key figure in gay homicides up until his demotion in 1978, Gilford's *Examiner* obituary corrects the record and refers to him as "the first San Francisco cop to mobilize the city's gay community to help catch a serial killer." Sanders recalled Gilford's impact on his investigations, saying,

A lot of cops didn't want to go into a gay bar back then, but Gil was comfortable with everyone. He showed me that if you treated everyone with respect, you would receive a lot more cooperation. He practiced the ultimate ideal of community policing—long before the term became popular.

Gilford's successes were recognized years before his death. Former mayor George Moscone appointed Gilford to his council on criminal justice in 1978, but preceded his new councilman in death when he was assassinated alongside Harvey Milk six months after Gilford started his new job. After Moscone's murder, Dianne Feinstein moved from the San Francisco Board of Supervisors to fill the position of acting mayor.

Moscone and Milk were murdered by former city supervisor Dan White. White went on to plead the infamous "Twinkie defense" to the jury. His actions, he claimed, came about because of depression—depression that was exacerbated by his change of diet from healthy foods to sugar-laden processed products, such as Twinkies and Coca-Cola. His saccharine psychological state, his lawyers argued, prevented the mental capacity to premeditate the murders. He was convicted of voluntary manslaughter rather than first-degree murder, a verdict that enraged many in San Francisco and across the country. After serving five years of his seven-year sentence, White was paroled in 1984. Less than two years later, back in San Francisco, White closed his garage, opened his car door, and started the engine. His body was found later in the day by his brother.

When Feinstein replaced Moscone after his assassination, she included Gilford as a deputy mayor under her administration, which continued for a decade until 1988. Gilford remained active in politics but never ran for office, choosing instead to align himself with campaigns that supported his policy goals.

Throughout his list of achievements, his work as the first Black homicide inspector in the SFPD was never forgotten, nor was his decision to leave the force and focus on the youth community and early crime prevention, education, and positive values—often through sports coaching. "The special thing about Rotea is he believed in a close family. He was a wonderful mentor to young people. His no-nonsense philosophy is what I appreciated. He didn't go for that politically correct stuff. He was old school—hard work, discipline, family, and loyalty—the basic virtues," as Dianne Feinstein put it after Gilford's death. The pair hadn't only talked politics; Gilford taught Feinstein how to play football, and the pair later attended San Francisco 49ers games and several Super Bowls. The friendship they forged endured until Gilford's death.

FOLLOWING GILFORD'S PASSING IN 1998, Sanders rose through the ranks of the San Francisco Police Department and served as its first Black police chief from 2002 to 2003. His status as the first officer to testify in court against systemic racism in the SFPD as a founder of the Officers for Justice was never forgotten, both by San Francisco civil rights advocates and by many in its police force. His achievements were impossible to ignore; he received eleven medals for meritorious service throughout the course of his forty-year career, making him one of the most decorated officers in SFPD history. His career ended, however, when questions about his detective work began. The fallout shook the very foundation of Sanders's legacy, leaving cracks that never fully closed.

Chief Prentice Earl Sanders.
Courtesy of the SFPD.

ON AUGUST 19, 1989, eighteen-year-old Roderick "Cooley" Shannon was shot and killed in the parking lot of a San Francisco convenience store. Two girls, aged fourteen and eleven, identified nineteen-year-old Antoine Goff and seventeen-year-old John Tennison as the assailants. On October 3, 1990, Goff and Tennison were sentenced to twenty-seven years to life and twenty-five years to life, respectively. After Tennison spent over fourteen years in prison, his guilty verdict was overturned in August 2003, the same year Sanders retired from his position as San Francisco's chief of police. The court found there were grave errors in both the investigation and prosecution of not only Tennison but Goff as well. Two superior court judges declared both men to be "factually innocent." Prentice Earl Sanders came to be a central figure in the bombshell story.

Sanders, alongside investigator Napoleon Hendrix, were the detectives assigned to Cooley's murder and now faced charges of hiding exculpatory evidence—including a post-trial taped confession by a man named Lovinsky Ricard. Ricard's was a name police were aware of; before Goff and Tennison ever entered the courtroom, an unnamed woman had pointed him out to the SFPD as a person of interest.

Sanders and Hendrix stood accused of burying Ricard's confession; it never saw the light of day in court, and both Goff and Tennison remained behind bars. And that wasn't all. There were indications that a $2,500 reward for information to solve the case had been offered—and Goff and Tennison's lawyers had never heard of it. If they had, the testimony of the young girls who identified Goff and Tennison as the men who killed Cooley would face even more scrutiny than it was already under. Their accusations stood alone as the single most important element of the prosecution's case; no physical evidence tying Goff or Tennison to Cooley's murder was ever found. The pair had plenty of reason to sue the city in federal court on the grounds of civil rights violations.

When U.S. District Judge Claudia Wilken released Tennison from prison, she agreed that police withheld key evidence from defense lawyers. Judge Wilken later tried the civil suits filed by both Goff and Tennison. Regarding the $2,500 reward, she concluded no money was ever actually paid to anyone, regardless of the reward's existence or nonexistence. The bigger issue to Judge Wilken was that there was a trial in the first place: "The prosecution's entire case was dependent upon the testimony of…two young girls whose eyewitness identifications of Tennison were questionable," she said.

Ricard's taped confession, Judge Wilken noted, was given to neither Sanders nor Hendrix but another investigator altogether. Jim Quadra, a private attorney hired by Sanders and Hendrix, argued against accusations by Tennison's attorneys that the partners had known about the tapes for seven months prior to their client's hearing for a new trial in May 1991. As for Ricard himself, he clung to the Fifth Amendment throughout the entirety of the civil case. Judge Wilken ruled the issues of both the reward and the confession be presented to a jury for resolution, if one was to be pursued. She felt the same about the woman who allegedly accused Ricard prior to Tennison's and Goff's trials. The City of San Francisco moved to settle the dispute. Tennison was eventually granted $4.5 million, and Goff received $2.9 million. These were not the last payments doled out to someone falsely convicted in a case Sanders and Hendrix oversaw.

On October 25, 2009, Napoleon Hendrix died at the age of seventy-eight. Just over a year later, the conviction of forty-year-old Caramad Conley was overturned. Conley spent eighteen years behind bars for the double murder of Roshawn Johnson and Charles Hughes in a drive-by shooting on April 8, 1989. Conley, at age eighteen, received two life sentences for the crime. Just as in Goff's and Tennison's trials, the prosecution relied on witness testimony for a conviction—and this time, Sanders knew Clifford Polk, who swore Conley confessed to him, had lied on the stand.

Polk, unbeknownst to the defense, was a paid police informant who worked for Sanders and had been in the witness protection program as a result of his testimony in another conviction. Polk was even provided with a house. Yet when he was asked under oath whether he had been compensated in any way, Polk denied it. Sanders was in the courtroom and witnessed the false testimony but did not intervene. When Conley sued the City of San Francisco, Sanders provided a deposition acknowledging that all of this did, in fact, occur—but due to his immunity as a law enforcement officer, he did nothing illegal. In 2014, two years after a failed attempt at suing Sanders directly, Conley was granted $3.5 million by the State of California.

On January 11, 2021, Prentice Earl Sanders died of kidney failure in a Burlingame assisted living facility at the age of eighty-three. The gap in time between the Goff, Tennison, and Conley scandals and Sanders's passing had exponentially mended his reputation. The press, the SFPD, and the general public seemed to have resolved any conflicting feelings about Sanders—or simply forgot they ever existed in the first place. In hindsight, Sanders's career as a detective comprises both hard-earned honor and well-deserved scrutiny—he was both a pioneer in changing the SFPD's discriminatory practices and a witness to questionable activities within that very same department.

SFPD chief William Scott said in a statement after Sanders's death, "He earned widespread respect from the diverse communities he served as a beat cop, homicide inspector, and member of the command staff. Yet he heroically risked his ascent through the ranks to remedy the injustices of racial bias"—racial bias that had included the cancellation of the annual SFPD Christmas party after Sanders and two other Black police officers first began their careers in the robbery detail. Eight years after that incident, when Gilford and Sanders called in for backup with a violent suspect in tow, a voice came over the radio and simply stated, "You don't have any buddies out here."

Sanders's SFPD career, while certainly the Goliath of his life, did not define him entirely. Following his death, numerous loved ones attested to his ability to overcome adversity in all its manifestations. In 2007, when Sanders coauthored *The Zebra Murders* with writer Bennett Cohen, the book served to both chronicle the Zebra case and take back control of his career narrative. Sanders had spent the years between the scandalous overturned convictions and the book's publication tucked away in Folsom, a little less than three hours from San Francisco. When it came time to unveil *The Zebra Murders*, Sanders returned to the city. Maybe, his supporters said, there was more to his story than had been portrayed by the media.

The book drew both supporters and detractors. The former included Brad Pitt, whose production company optioned the story for a movie adaptation. The latter did not focus on Sanders's detective work but rather seethed with decades-long resentment over his legal action against the SFPD. His victory over the discriminatory practices within the department—the crown jewel of his legacy—still soured the mouths of several former officers. In 2007, retired deputy chief Kevin Mullen complained to the *San Francisco Chronicle* that Sanders's court testimony was an act of "opportunistic ingratitude....He goes on, as he has forever, complaining of how he has been used and abused by the very organization which made him what he became. It's disgraceful." A brief overview of press interviews with members of the SFPD during the original trial—in 1973, over thirty years prior to Mullen's quote—echoes the same sentiment throughout headlines and columns. So much had changed, and so much had not.

In the end, Sanders was remembered by friends and family not for his job, but for his spirit. His son, Marcus Sanders, told the *San Francisco Chronicle*, "My dad was a renaissance man. He was a caring father, and he had an indomitable smile. No matter what came at him, he had that smile."

Chapter 27

ON THE HEELS OF JUSTICE

On February 26, 2019, Investigative Bureau Commander Greg McEachern stepped up to a microphone at SFPD headquarters. Seated in front of him was a small number of reporters. Beside him, propped on a pedestal, was a presentation board that included the 1975 composite sketch of the Doodler, alongside a 2018 age progression image. Above the two drawings, in big bold lettering, were the words "$100,000 REWARD." Someone had been digging through the yellowed pages of the Doodler files.

McEachern recapped the timeline of the Doodler Murders and the attacks on three survivors. He reiterated much of what Gilford and Sanders had originally told the press of the connection between the homicides and the attempted murders; the surviving victims were all white, gay men, as the murdered were; both those who lived and those who died were patrons of the same or similar nightlife locations.

McEachern then introduced an audio recording of the original 911 call made to police to report finding Gerald's body on the shoreline of Ocean Beach. The voice sounds somewhat high-pitched and delicate but far from hysterical. As the person reports the body's location, the street name "Ulloa" is mispronounced at first. Rather than the correct "you-LOW-ah," the caller initially says "uh-LOW-ah." McEachern did not note if this was of any significance, though many criminal profilers would argue it is. If the caller was a local or a frequent visitor to Ocean Beach, there would likely be no confusion as to the proper pronunciation of the street name.

Left: 2018 age progression sketch of the Doodler, *Courtesy of the SFPD.*

Below: Members of the press photograph the SFPD's $100,000 reward for information leading to the capture of the Doodler. *Courtesy of the SFPD.*

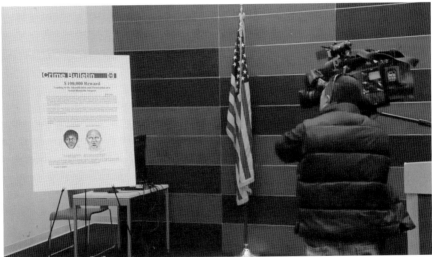

Gerald was found nearly washed out to sea—the caller would have had to be walking directly on the shoreline to see his body in the dark. Was the caller an outsider who came to Ocean Beach to stalk his victims? Or was it someone new to cruising the area who stumbled on the horrifying scene and wanted to report it but feared going public, just as three survivors of the Doodler had? As of 2022, no evidence has been made public that can help differentiate between these two theories.

Though original investigators told the press of three suspects they looked into during the original Doodler investigation (the psychiatric patient of Dr. Priest, Lawrence Robinson, and the unnamed man picked up at a Tenderloin gay bar while drawing and carrying a butcher knife), McEachern only mentioned one. The tale of the "patient" was presented

Commander Greg McEachern speaks to the press at a February 6, 2019 briefing on the Doodler case. *Courtesy of the SFPD.*

to the press, but it was clear one thing was missing from the case file: the psychiatrist's report. McEachern told the press the SFPD also needed help finding the psychiatrist himself, as the only record they have of his report is a note made by Gilford, buried in his papers and lacking specific details or contact information. It's quite possible the name "Priest" isn't even accurate, as it is documented not by the psychiatrist but by Gilford, who might have misheard or misspelled the name.

The Diplomat is the only victim who is still alive as of 2022. The other two, only identified as a "nationally-known entertainer" and a powerful "local figure," both left San Francisco after the attacks, refusing to cooperate with police. Before his murder, Harvey Milk talked to the press of the survivors' decision, saying, "I can understand their position. I can visualize the pressure society has put on them."

While progress has majorly changed public acceptance of the LGBTQ community, it is not enough for the Diplomat to reveal the details of the darkest night of his life. What's more, the killer might still be alive. His willingness to return to the Diplomat's apartment building after an attempted murder shows he does not fear the victim—and didn't think twice about the attempt on the Diplomat's life. The Doodler might be dead; he might be well past his physical prime—but try to tell that to survivors of such violent attacks, who suffer lifetime ramifications from the experience. The Diplomat's silence may be born of valid fear—one no one should ever endure.

It was the press's turn to ask questions of Commander McEachern. Could "Priest" be not a last name but a reference to a Catholic priest? McEachern did not think so. What about the reasons behind the renewed interest in the case? Fresh on everyone's mind was the April 24, 2018 arrest of Joseph James DeAngelo, also known as the Golden State Killer. DeAngelo committed at least thirteen murders, fifty-one rapes, and 120 burglaries from the early 1970s through at least 1986, and a combination of independent investigators and cutting-edge DNA technology finally brought the septuagenarian to justice. Was the reopened Doodler investigation related? McEachern replied,

> *The interest in this case now is no different than it is for all of our other cold cases. We take a look at cases that we believe are solvable, and cases that the victim has never had justice in. And last year, when the Golden State Killer was apprehended, we went back and looked at all other crimes, especially serial crimes, that were occurring in the past. We know that in the 1970s, this was gripping the gay community in San Francisco, and so Inspector Dan Cunningham reopened all the cases that were involved at that time to see if we could identify who that is so that we can get closure for those victims and hopefully make an arrest in those cases.*

Then came the key question at the forefront of every cold case investigator's mind: Was there DNA evidence? McEachern said yes. Several samples were submitted to the crime lab over the course of 2018, but results had not come in yet. As of 2022, they still have not. "At this time, we have to wait for the crime lab to give us the information back, so I don't have a timeline," McEachern told reporters in 2019.

What of the main person of interest, the man who allegedly confessed to his psychiatrist? Was he still around? "He is," McEachern said with a knowing nod. Not only was he still alive, but he was brought in from his current home in the East Bay for additional questioning in 2018. Did he look like the man in the age progression sketch of the Doodler? McEachern replied, "I'm not going to comment on whether or not the person of interest's sketch is the same or at least similar." With that, McEachern and Inspector Cunningham stepped offstage to speak quietly with lingering journalists.

The story reached several international news sources but didn't make the same headlines the search for the Golden State Killer had in the mid-2010s, while DeAngelo still remained in the shadows. Yet the Doodler case has some similar elements: those who survived his attacks provided police with a description and, most importantly—the Doodler left behind his DNA.

DeAngelo was found by investigators who ran crime scene DNA through a personal genomics website named GEDmatch. The site serves as a giant database of publicly submitted DNA from those in search of blood relatives or an ethnicity analysis. Has this been done with the Doodler's DNA? As of 2022, SFPD has gone no further than to say its own crime lab is still processing its analysis results. It hadn't only been DNA that put DeAngelo behind bars, however. Pressure from both the public and the press mounted for years, pushing the Golden State Killer case to the forefront of several California jurisdictions' cold case investigations.

Since the 2019 press conference, one major piece of information has been officially released: there was a potential sixth Doodler homicide. The case is that of Warren Andrews, a man discovered on April 27, 1975, near Lands End, his head severely battered. A few weeks later, Harald Gullberg's body was found close by.

Andrews was not the victim of a homicide—yet. After around two months in a coma, Andrews was declared dead in his home in Seattle, surrounded by loved ones. Key evidence was left behind at the crime scene—including the murder weapons. A rock, tree branch, and handkerchief, all covered in blood, were never analyzed, though; they were lost to time, along with the other physical evidence gathered. As of 2022, SFPD has not located any of it.

If Andrews was indeed a victim of the Doodler, he died differently than the others—none had been bludgeoned. There is no public evidence as to whether Andrews's murderer had a knife with him—but in February 2022, Inspector Cunningham theorized to this writer that a knife could have been lost in a struggle and then picked back up by the killer before he left the scene.

Andrews also fits the Doodler victim profile; he was white, almost certainly gay, and killed in a common hookup location. The fifty-two-year-old lawyer shared many similarities with the Doodler's other victims. His case is now included in the active investigation headed by Inspector Cunningham.

When it comes to the murder of George Gilbert at the Fox Plaza shortly after the Doodler attacked two victims there, Cunningham confirmed to this writer that, while he cannot fully rule out a connection, he has reviewed the Gilbert murder and does not believe it is related. No further details were provided.

What of Lawrence Robinson, the man Inspector Dave Toschi named as a potential Doodler suspect in 1977? Cunningham told this writer that while he couldn't recall specific details or definitively rule out Robinson, he feels strongly Robinson is not the Doodler. He also stressed that many men have been considered as potential persons of interest in this case—while the patient of Dr. Priest is most heavily focused on by both police and the press, he is not the only man investigators are thoroughly looking into.

With regard to the blond white man who stole Jae Stevens's car shortly after his murder, Cunningham confirmed to this writer that he does not believe the incident to be related—rather, it was likely a separate act committed by an opportunistic criminal who happened to be in the right place at the right time. Without the Hayward Police Department's files on the incident, the full details of that night remain unclear.

In February 2022, this writer received confirmation that the SFPD is looking deeper into an alternate theory about the murders—one that involves few, if any, of the fabled drawings. This theory is supported by the documented public awareness in the gay community of the Doodler Murders.

While San Francisco is a big city, its neighborhoods become small villages of their own, and many nightlife patrons frequently cross paths—in reality, the scene is only so big. The possibility that the killer could cast the same lure six different times within two years may exist, but Cunningham finds it questionable. Citizen patrols were working day and night to keep the LGBTQ community safe on the streets; Cunningham himself recalls stopping at a donut shop near Eighteenth and Castro Streets one night and hearing the yells of a drunken assault. Whistles pierced the air, growing shriller as the Butterfly Brigade closed in. Was this really where the Doodler would so lethally succeed?

The artist arrested with a knife while sketching in the Tenderloin was one of two Black males repeatedly called in to police (and cleared) as potential Doodler suspects after the SFPD released the composite sketch and described the Diplomat's nearly fatal encounter. The Tenderloin artist reached a breaking point—how many times would he need to be interviewed and released in connection to the Doodler case? These multiple arrests show that citizens were actively on the lookout for the Doodler and often reported possible sightings to law enforcement.

Even though several of the Doodler's victims were last seen alive in the Castro, a significant gap in time lies between the witness sightings and the body discoveries. Cunningham pointed out to this writer that there was ample opportunity for the Doodler victims to encounter their killer in an entirely separate location from where they were last seen. Ocean Beach, Golden Gate Park, and Lands End were all well-established cruising grounds for the gay community—the Doodler Murders occurred years before the AIDS epidemic, which closed the highly trafficked bathhouses and public restrooms that could have easily played host to some of the victims. Could Gerald, Jae, Klaus, Harald, and possibly Warren have all met the Doodler not in the Castro but, instead, near the crime scenes?

The SFPD maintains that the dead are linked through their murder locations, their shared ethnicity and sexual identity, the lack of robbery, and the rage-fueled stab wounds—not witnesses who could attest to the artist, the pickup, the Black man. Those details only emerged after three survivors told police of the horrific attacks perpetrated by a man who remains unidentified—publicly. There are enough similarities between the assault survivors and the murder victims for the SFPD to feel confident in a connection, but this writer must note that these similarities are not enough to prove that the Doodler is the same man who attacked the Diplomat, the "well-known entertainer," and the local public figure. If no one can attest to seeing Gerald, Jae, Klaus, Frederick, or Harald with a man matching the description of the Diplomat's attacker—or seeing any of them with a sketch artist on or before the night of their deaths—then the possibility that at least two separate men are involved cannot be ruled out without the completion of the crime scene DNA analysis or new witness testimony. A thorough look at the cases of Randy Kraft, Patrick Kearney, and William Bonin illustrates the major hurdles law enforcement can encounter during their investigations when multiple murderers target the same demographic simultaneously. The legend of the Doodler drawing for his murder victims, as was experienced by the Diplomat, has not been proven by the current investigation—if anything, its likeliness has begun to weaken. The Diplomat told police the Doodler drew pictures of animals, not portraits of patrons. Gilford and Sanders told the press they had never recovered drawings of any kind. Was the story simply urban legend? Folklore conjured to protect the vulnerable, strung through the grapevine of the Castro? The "Freeway Killer" moniker came to belong to three unrelated killers—will the title of "The Doodler" prove similar?

WHOEVER KILLED GERALD CAVANAGH, the first known victim in this murder series, would have required a basic plan if he wanted to avoid the repercussions of his crime. He would have been blood-soaked following the murder—how did he escape unnoticed before police were called to the scene, just in time to pull Gerald's body back from the sea? Cunningham has a theory—one that can't be reached without a knowledge of the landscape of San Francisco's Sunset District in the 1970s. Those were the last years during which a seawall and a pedestrian tunnel located on Ocean Beach at the end of Taraval Street stood, feet away from the crime scene, before both were dismantled and forgotten. It wasn't until the rubble began to surface among the sand in 2016 that the city was reminded of the concrete colossi, originally built in the 1920s. At the time of the Doodler Murders, the tunnel would have made for a perfect exit route, doubling as a discreet location for the killer to clean himself up and change clothing. If he was indeed the same man who later left three survivors, perhaps the escape from Ocean Beach had simply become too easy—which made the choice to up the ante and attack victims in their own homes a natural progression of his modus operandi.

If the killer did indeed become comfortable taking lives in his victims' own homes, then he was not the only one. The murders of Stig Berlin, George Gilbert, Claude DeMott, Richard Trapnell, Robert O'Shields, and so many more gay men who were viciously stabbed to death remain unsolved. The Doodler was not the only man hunting throughout the Castro in the mid-1970s for sport—and he is not the only one who has eluded law enforcement for over four decades.

In 2012, SFPD cold case files inspector Pat Correa reopened the investigations of Barbarella Vasquez and Lisa Yancey, the trans women who were murdered in the Tenderloin in 1975, the same year the Doodler killed Frederick Capin and Harald Gullberg. Correa came out of retirement in 2011 on a federal grant to give San Francisco's unsolved murders a fresh eye.

Along with Barbarella's and Lisa's murders, another killing was also being analyzed by Correa: that of thirty-seven-year-old Stig Berlin. When his body was found at his Hyde Street apartment on February 17, 1974, it was covered by the press less than Barbarella's and Lisa's deaths. He was found stabbed to death, his home left in complete disarray.

A September 5, 2012 *Bay Area Reporter* article covered the reinvestigations and interviewed Correa on the challenges she faced with the cases. The biggest hurdle, it seemed, was locating anyone who knew Berlin, Vasquez, or Yancey. "I can't get to them, because they're no longer here. That's the biggest challenge right now," she said. With regard to DNA evidence, Correa hoped the crime lab would be able to pull something out of the past. However, without any new witnesses, even a viable DNA sample might not be enough to solve the case—just as two sets of fingerprints recovered from Yancey's apartment hadn't been. Correa knew she needed a more detailed picture of Berlin, Vasquez, and Yancey's killer or killers in order to move their cases toward closure. "It's like working a big jigsaw puzzle for me," Correa told the *Bay Area Reporter* of her search for justice for the victims. As of 2022, the SFPD has not found it.

IN SEPTEMBER 2021, MAJOR Crimes Sergeant Young of the San Mateo County Sheriff's Office provided this writer with an update on the San Mateo murders investigation. The San Mateo Sheriff's Office was in the midst of reviewing all of its cold case homicides, particularly those involving unidentified victims—including John Doe #78-2, found along Tunitas Creek Road. Original press coverage of the San Mateo murders in the late 1970s linked Doe's murder with those of Tom Goodman, Ronald Young, Daniel Joseph Oller, and Raymond Oscar Wilson. Was this still law enforcement's position? Sergeant Young confirmed the murders still appear to be the work of one killer. Was it David Likens?

While Sergeant Young would like to reveal a current suspect name, there is a major roadblock: one of the victims is a John Doe. Young said,

> I want to make sure that in all these cases, the victim's families have been notified. We are looking at unidentified remains, plus we're looking at homicides, and I want to make sure all of our numbers match and all of these people, all of their families, are identified first, before anything goes out. [Because] if they read it somehow, or a family member reads it, and goes, "What's going on here? Why did no one come and talk to us?"—that would be the worst thing for us to happen, is that they read that in the paper somewhere.

Young maintains the original press coverage of a focused, hardworking team of investigators assigned to the cases in the 1970s is accurate, saying, "I will tell you, back then the detectives, they did a great job." The evidence collected in the original investigation supports the current police theory: "We think these people were picked up in the city [of San Francisco] and brought out [to San Mateo County]. We don't believe they were hitchhiking. It looks like it may have been some sort of sexual encounter, and then this guy did what he did."

While Likens cannot be publicly named in the reopened investigation of the San Mateo murders as of 2022, Sergeant Young did offer, "We believe that the suspect is going to be one person who is deceased." As Likens hanged himself after he was formally charged and about to be tried for homicide in the San Mateo murder cases, this is the closest thing to confirmation that Sergeant Young can offer.

The San Mateo murder series does not include all of the unsolved homicides and other John Does that were found dumped in the area—during the 1970s, multiple bodies were spread throughout San Mateo County and have yet to be identified.

On May 10, 1974, the legs and torso of John Doe #74-407 were found at the Linda Mar State Beach in Pacifica by a passing jogger. The man wore Levi Strauss jeans and white briefs. John Doe #75-936 was found a quarter mile south of Huddart Park on Kings Mountain Road in San Mateo on October 13, 1975. Nine to twelve years of age, he was wearing a dark-blue sweater jacket with a striped liner and size 7–7.5 brown boots. He also carried a wooden rosary with a back-to-front clasp bearing the word "Italy."

John Doe #78-03's partial skeletal remains were found under the Doran Bridge by hikers on December 31, 1978. A year prior, on December 18, 1977, another hiker found the decomposed torso and thighs of a young male of unknown age, known as John Doe #77-1048, at the Point Montara Lighthouse. Around his waist was a strip of denim. On March 6, 1984, John Doe #84-7, a white male approximately twenty to thirty years of age, was found along Guadalupe Road, nude and stripped of his property. John Doe #83-26 was found partially clothed on Lower Pillar Point in Half Moon Bay on November 26, 1983. Police theorized he came to the area from the Tenderloin district of San Francisco.

Both law enforcement and independent investigators are aware of the multitude of homicides and cases with unknown causes of death—some potentially committed by serial killers and some not—that were occurring in the area at the time. Since then, several of these murderers have been caught and some of their victims identified. One serial killer had visited the Bay Area and its surrounding towns multiple times for his work as a successful computer programmer: Randy Steven Kraft. This writer asked if he was ever considered in any of San Mateo's other cold case homicides. Sergeant Young had never heard of Kraft—and said it sounded worth looking into.

> *Trust me, if Randy Kraft wasn't associated with any of this before, I will now be looking at him for other homicides....Unfortunately, back then, there were a lot of bodies that were dumped. But we'll start looking at Kraft. Because we need to go back and resubmit DNA, resubmit evidence.*

OVER TIME, CALIFORNIA'S JURISDICTIONS have become littered with unsolved homicides. Loved ones lack justice; some families are left to assume their son or brother just up and left one day without notice. Birthdays come and go, holidays pass, grandchildren are born—but time moves at a different speed for those left behind. Years fly by, yet life is also perpetually fixed in that one moment, when everything changed.

As cold case inspectors, journalists, and the curious-at-large learn more of these murders, the odds increase in favor of justice. Among dust-covered filing boxes and the fog of memory lie the solutions to so many of these cases. In the search for the killers who walked free from their crimes, hope remains.

JANUARY 27, 2022 MARKED forty-eight years to the day since Gerald Earl Cavanagh's body nearly washed out to sea. The San Francisco Police Department once again gathered the press—this time to announce the reward for information leading to the closure of the Doodler case had doubled to $200,000. Detective Cunningham told the *San Francisco Chronicle* he felt the SFPD is "closer than ever to solving it."

ACKNOWLEDGEMENTS

I would like to first and foremost thank Melissa Honrath for entrusting me with her memories and photographs of her brother, Joseph "Jae" Stevens. Dr. Allan Branson, thank you for providing invaluable insight into many of the topics discussed in this book. To Sergeant Alan Levy of the San Francisco Police Department, thank you for responding to my queries on dozens of cases. Thank you to Isaac Fellman and the entire GLBT Historical Society for their guidance and wisdom throughout my research. To Lieutenant Dan Cunningham of the SFPD, thank you for taking the time to discuss the Doodler Murders with me and for your dedication to justice in this case.

My deepest gratitude to the *San Francisco Sentinel* and the *Bay Area Reporter* for providing the overwhelming majority of press coverage available on these cases—without those publications, this book would not exist. Thank you to the San Francisco History Center at the San Francisco Public Library for maintaining such vital archives. Thank you to Kevin Fagan of the *San Francisco Chronicle* for his investigative reporting on the Doodler Murders and for bringing this case back to the headlines. To Malcolm Lanzin and the Equality Forum, thank you for keeping the message of Dr. Anonymous alive. Thank you to Sergeant Young of the San Mateo County Sheriff's Office for the encouragement—it meant a lot.

Much of the reference data in this book was provided by the dedicated team at the National Center for Analysis of Violent Crime. Thank you to the NCAVC, as well as the Behavioral Analysis Unit at the FBI for their cornerstone contributions to the study of serial killers. Thank you to Bennett Cohen for writing *The Zebra Murders* and taking the time to answer my questions. My deepest appreciation to Dr. Eric W. Hickey for advising me on the importance of good mental health while researching and writing about serial homicide.

Thank you to Cara Moore for permitting me to feature her beautiful photograph on the cover of this book. Thank you to Jason Bowman, Carol Highsmith, Terri Meyer Boake, Harry Goodman, and Alex Bierwagen for their photographs throughout these pages.

My deepest appreciation to my editor, Laurie Krill, and my copyeditor, Zoe Ames, who helped make the writing of my first book such a meaningful experience. To the entire Arcadia Publishing and The History Press team, thank you for believing in this story—and in me.

To my loved ones, thank you for so much more than I could ever put to the page. Thank you to my aunt, Beth Schultz, for inspiring me with her courage and kindness. Thank you to Caitlin Sposato for staying. To my great-aunt, Olga Collie, thank you for always making sure I had a book to read when I came over for a visit. Thank you to Matty Dowlen and his family for always standing by me in both victory and defeat.

This book is also for my grandparents, Kay and Sam Zaliznock, who never missed an episode of *Unsolved Mysteries*. To the rest of my extended, loud, and loving family—I hope I've made you proud.

BIBLIOGRAPHY

Alfred, Randy. "Anti-Gay Violence, Any Time, Any Place." *San Francisco Sentinel*, June 30, 1977.

————. "Patrolling the Streets." *San Francisco Sentinel*, December 16, 1976.

Alison, Emily, Laurence John Alison and David Canter. "The Organized/Disorganized Typology of Serial Murder: Myth or Model?" *Psychology Public Policy and Law* 10 (September 2004): 293–320.

American Psychological Association. *Task Force on Appropriate Therapeutic Responses to Sexual Orientation*. (2009): 26–53.

Associated Press. "Prentice 'Earl' Sanders, San Francisco's First Black Police Chief, Dies at 83." *Los Angeles Times*, January 11, 2021.

Bajko, Matthew. "Death Row's 'Scorecard Killer,' a.k.a. 'Freeway Killer,' Randy Kraft, Speaks." *Pride* (Los Angeles, CA), November 3, 2016.

Bay Area Reporter. "Finding the Answers: Beatings Continue." February 19, 1976.

————. "Gay Action Moves to Curb Violence." November 24, 1976.

————. "Gay Crime Study Slated." December 22, 1977.

————. "Human Psychologists." September 15, 1977.

————. "Murderers at Large in Tenderloin." April 17, 1975.

————. "NGTF Resents Coverage of Trash Bag Killings." July 21, 1977.

————. "Police Seek Help in Gay Murders." October 26, 1978.

————. "San Mateo Slayings." October 26, 1978.

————. "Trash Bag Murders." July 7, 1977.

Beardemphl, W.E. "Editorial Comments." *San Francisco Sentinel*, December 5, 1974.

Berkeley (CA) Gazette. "Rich Steel Executive Murdered in S.F." December 9, 1976.

Berton, Justin. "Free for First Time in 18 Years." *San Francisco Chronicle*, January 13, 2011.

Bismark (CA) Tribune. "Assault Victims Won't Testify." July 8, 1977.

Blackston, Elliott. "Off the Beat." *San Francisco Sentinel*, July 18, 1974.

———. "Off the Beat." *San Francisco Sentinel*, September 26, 1974.

———. "Off the Beat." *San Francisco Sentinel*, April 24, 1975.

———. "Off the Beat." *San Francisco Sentinel*, November 7, 1974.

———. "Off the Beat." *San Francisco Sentinel*, September 12, 1974.

Boldenweck, Bill. "Five Linked Slayings Spark Fear of More Gay Murders." *San Francisco Examiner*, October 13, 1978.

———. "Special Detail Delves into San Mateo Murders." *San Francisco Examiner*, October 18, 1978.

Branson, Allan. *The Anonymity of African American Serial Killers: A Continuum of Negative Imagery from Slavery to Prisons*. Monee, IL: self-published, 2015.

———. "African American Serial Killers: Over-Represented Yet Underacknowledged." *Howard Journal of Crime and Justice* (February 2013): 1–18.

———. Interviews with the author, 2021–22.

Burgess, Ace A. "Sex-Killing Suspects 'Nice Guys' to Neighbors." *Press-Telegram (Long Beach, CA)*, July 7, 1977.

Cahill, Sean, and Jason Cianciotto. *Youth in the Crosshairs: The Third Wave of Ex-Gay Activism*. New York: National Gay and Lesbian Task Force Policy Institute, 2007.

Californians (Salinas, CA). "'Trashbag Slayer' Gets Life Sentence." December 22, 1977.

City and County of San Francisco Coroner's Office. Autopsy Report of Frederick Elmer Capin. May 12, 1975.

———. Autopsy Report of George J. Gilbert. October 1, 1975.

———. Autopsy Report of Gerald Earl Cavanagh. January 30, 1974.

———. Autopsy Report of Harald Gullberg. July 6, 1975.

———. Autopsy Report of Joseph Stevens. June 25, 1974.

Contra Costa (CA) Times. "Victim Was Port Costa Resident." November 1, 1978.

Coté, John. "S.F. Expected to Pay $3.5 Million in Double-Murder Wrongful Conviction." *San Francisco Chronicle*, July 12, 2014.

———. "Wrongfully Convicted S.F. Man Likely to Get $3.5 Million Dollars." *San Francisco Chronicle*, July 14, 2014.

Crewdson, John M. "Coast Killings: A Bizarre Case Widens." *New York Times*, July 11, 1977.

Cunningham, Dan (SFPD inspector). Interviews with the author, 2022.

Daily News (Port Angeles, WA). Obituary of Frederick E. Capin. August 15, 1975.

Daily Press (Victorville, CA). "Parolee Charged in Murders." December 15, 1978.

Dobbin, Muriel. "'Violence Hotline' Begun on Coast." *Baltimore (MD) Sun*, 1977.

Downs, Jim. *Stand By Me: The Forgotten History of Gay Liberation*. New York: Basic Books, 2016.

Edwards, Mark. "Letter to the Editor." *San Francisco Chronicle*, January 29, 1976.

Egelko, Bob. "Freed Inmate's Compensation Appeal Denied." *San Francisco Chronicle*, October 18, 2007.

———. "Freed Prisoner Loses Bid for Compensation—Court Says Man Hasn't Proved He's Innocent." *San Francisco Chronicle*, June 30, 2007.

———. "Wrongly Convicted Rarely Get State Case." *San Francisco Chronicle*, February 20, 2018.

Ellerbrok, Ariane, and Kevin Haggerty. "The Social Study of Serial Killers." *Criminal Justice and the Coalition* 86: (2013): 1–4.

Eureka (CA) Times-Standard. "'Doodler' Remains at Large in Bay Area." July 8, 1977.

Fagan, Kevin. "Cold Case Heats Up as SF Police Release New Sketch of Killer in 1970s Gay Stabbing Spree." *San Francisco Chronicle*, February 7, 2019.

———. "The Doodler: A Sixth Victim? And Maybe More Outside the Bay Area." *San Francisco Chronicle*, April 27, 2021.

———. "The Doodler: Four Murders. A Pattern. The Cops Are Catching On." *San Francisco Chronicle*, March 30, 2021.

———. "Police Say They're 'Closer Than Ever' to Solving One of San Francisco's Most Notorious Serial Killer Cold Cases." *San Francisco Chronicle*, January 27, 2022.

Fallon, James. *The Psychopath Inside: A Neuroscientist's Personal Journey into the Dark Side of the Brain*. New York: Penguin, 2014.

Feinstein, Dianne. "Candidate Statement." October 1975.

Freedom Newspapers, Inc. v. Superior Court, 186 Cal. App.3d 1102 (4th District, California, 1986).

Fresno (CA) Bee. "San Franciscan Man Named in Gay Murders." December 14, 1978.

Goldman, David C. "Letter to the Editor." *Bay Area Reporter*, April 3, 1975.

Goodkind, Mike. "LA Area Pair Quizzed in Up To 43 Murders." *Fresno (CA) Bee*, July 4, 1977.

Hall, Stephen. "New Kind of Chase for S.F. Cop." *San Francisco Chronicle*, May 5, 1978.

Hardman, Paul D. "Gay Man Murdered at Home." *Bay Area Reporter*, July 8, 1976.

———. "Murder Victim Bled to Death." *Bay Area Reporter*, October 28, 1976.

———. "San Jose Police Refuse to Protect Gays from Murder Attempt." *Bay Area Reporter*, April 29, 1976.

———. "Special Investigation Squad Formed by S.F. Police." *Bay Area Reporter*, May 13, 1976.

Hartmann, Paul-Francis. "The Fall of David Toschi." *Bay Area Reporter*, August 3, 1978.

Hemmelgarn, Seth. "SFPD Seeks Killers in Cold Cases." *Bay Area Reporter*, September 5, 2012.

Hickey, Eric W. Interview with the author, 2021.

———. *Serial Murderers and Their Victims*. Belmont, CA: Wadsworth, 2010.

Hicks, Jerry. "'78 Deaths Recounted as Kraft Trial Resumes." *Los Angeles Times*, November 1, 1988.

Honrath, Melissa. Interviews with the author, 2021–22.

Independent (Long Beach, CA). "Body Identified as Lost 'Hondo.'" June 9, 1977.

———. "Door-to-Door Hunt for Lennox Boy, 5." August 26, 1974.

Independent (Richmond, CA). "Family Tragedy." November 12, 1976.

"In Memoriam: Jae Stevens." *Drag Magazine* 4, no. 16, 1974.

Jackson, Don. "Surgery for Gays?! Psychosurgery Advocate at Helm of Justice." *Bay Area Reporter*, July 11, 1973.

Jenkins, Philip. "Catch Me Before I Kill More: Seriality as Modern Monstrosity." *Cultural Analysis* 3 (2002): 1–17.

Jennings, Duffy. "Strange Turn in the Zodiac Case." *San Francisco Chronicle*, July 11, 1978.

———. "Tracking Down a Killer." *San Francisco Chronicle*, April 2, 1974.

Johns, Dave. "Another Case of Murder." *San Francisco Sentinel*, April 24, 1975.

———. "Police Checking Grisly Case." *San Francisco Sentinel*, August 14, 1975.

———. "Police Checking Out Tenderloin Murders." *San Francisco Sentinel*, April 10, 1975.

Julie Stevens v. Superior Ct. No. A89-00201 (Contra Costa County, 1990).

Keppel, Robert D. *Signature Killers: Interpreting the Calling Cards of the Serial Murderer*. New York: Pocket Books, 1997.

Kistler, Robert. "Mother Pleads for Return of Son: 'He's All I've Got.'" *Los Angeles Times*, August 31, 1974.

Kuehl, Peter, and Don Wegars. "The Mystery Witness in S.F. Gay Murders." *San Francisco Chronicle*, July 9, 1977.

Lagos, Marisa. "$7.5 Million Payout Likely in Misconduct." *San Francisco Chronicle*, July 28, 2009.

Lee, Charles. "22nd Unsolved Case: Actor Killed." *San Francisco Sentinel*, December 9, 1976.

———. "Castro Case Goes to Trial." *San Francisco Sentinel*, October 9, 1975.

———. "Cobs Nab 3 in Murders." *San Francisco Sentinel*, December 16, 1976.

———. "Gay Karate Classes Develop Confidence." *San Francisco Sentinel*, March 25, 1976.

———. "Gay Murders Defy Statistics." *San Francisco Sentinel*, December 16, 1976.

———. "More Arrests in Gay Murders." *San Francisco Sentinel*, January 13, 1977.

———. "Mutilated Body Identified." *San Francisco Sentinel*, December 30, 1976.

———. "Police Ask Help with Murder Case." *San Francisco Sentinel*, October 21, 1976.

———. "SFPD Announces Us 'Unstable.'" *San Francisco Sentinel*, 1975.

———. "SFPD Checking Tenderloin Murder, Questioning Suspect in 'Doodler' Case." *San Francisco Sentinel*, January 25, 1976.

———. "SFPD Describes Suspect in Murder Cases." *San Francisco Sentinel*, November 6, 1975.

———. "SFPD Pronounces Us 'Unstable.'" *San Francisco Sentinel*, August 1, 1974.

———. "Special Squad Tackles Murders." *San Francisco Sentinel*, May 20, 1976.

Lee, Henry K. "Freed Man Files Suit, Saying City Hid Truth." *San Francisco Chronicle*, February 1, 2012.

Lester, David. *Serial Killers: The Insatiable Passion*. Philadelphia: Charles Press, 1995.

Levy, Alan (SFPD sergeant). Interview with the author, 2021.

Lewis, Gregory. "Rotea Gilford, Former Deputy Mayor, Dies at 70." *San Francisco Examiner*, March 16, 1998.

Lindsey, Robert. "11th Possible Victim Is Identified in Multiple Murder Case on Coast." *New York Times*, July 7, 1977.

Los Angeles Herald Examiner. "Transients Held in Slaying." December 11, 1976.

Los Angeles Times. "Body Found in Brush Believed to Be That of Missing Boy, 5." October 14, 1974.

———. "Hunt Pressed for 5-Year-Old Boy Missing Since Saturday." August 27, 1974.

———. "Police Ask Public to Help Find Missing 8-Year-Old." April 11, 1977.

Maatz, Larry. "Vice Cops Net a Male 'Escort' Ring." *San Francisco Examiner*, March 9, 1979.

Martin, Reagan. *Young, Queer, and Dead: A Biography of San Francisco's Most Overlooked Serial Killer, The Doodler*. Anaheim, CA: Absolute Crime Press, 2019.

Martinez, Don. "Grisly Scene in E. Bay—Mother Gone, Kin Held." *San Francisco Examiner*, October 11, 1974.

McDougal, Dennis. *Angel of Darkness: The True Story of Randy Kraft and the Most Heinous Murder Spree of the Century*. New York: Warner Books, 1991.

Mendenhall, George. "Another Tenderloin Murder." *Bay Area Reporter*, February 5, 1976.

———. "Castro Patrol Blasted in Examiner Editorial." *Bay Area Reporter*, July 7, 1977.

———. "Chief Supports Gay Cops." *Bay Area Reporter*, February 5, 1976.

———. "Exclusive: Police Chief Gain Speaks Out." *Bay Area Reporter*, January 22, 1976.

Migden, Carole. "What About Crime in the Castro?" *Bay Area Reporter*, March 31, 1994.

Modesto (CA) Bee. "2 Suspects Arraigned in LA's 'Trash Bag Murders.'" July 6, 1977.

Morris, Charles Lee. "Hold Two on Murder Slaying." *San Francisco Sentinel*, July 28, 1977.

Morton, Robert J., Jennifer M. Tillman and Stephanie J. Gaines. *Serial Murders: Pathways for Investigations.* Quantico, VA: National Center for the Analysis of Violent Crime, Behavioral Analysis Unit at the Federal Bureau of Investigations: 2014.

Nellis, Ashley. *The Color of Justice: Racial and Ethnic Disparity in State Prisons.* Sentencing Project, October 2021.

New York Times. "3 More Bodies of Missing Youths Identified by California Authorities." July 12, 1977.

Oakland Tribune. "Older Sister Fights Off Grim Attack." October 12, 1974.

———. "S.F. Cops Hunt for a Killer." December 9, 1976.

———. "Suspects Held in Kitchen Slaying." December 14, 1976.

The People of California v. David Allen Likens No. A-129103 (California, 1974).

The People of California v. Kraft, 5 P.3d 68, 23 Cal. 4th 978 (California, 2000).

Petaluma (CA) Argus-Courier. "SF Police Arrest Man." January 13, 1977.

———. "Two SF Killings Reported." December 13, 1976.

Press-Telegram (Long Beach, CA). "76 Hollywood Killings May Be Linked to Pair." July 7, 1977.

Ramirez, Raul. "Convicted L.A. Mutilation-Murderer Now Jailed Here on Same Charge." *San Francisco Examiner*, December 14, 1978.

Redd, Wyatt. "The Story of Patrick Kearney, The Genuis Serial Killer Who Had Sex with His Victims After Murdering Them." *All That's Interesting*, June 14, 2018.

Redondo (CA) Reflex. "Dog Hairs Link Men to Slayings." July 6, 1977.

———. "Missing Venice Boy, 8, Reported Seen Sunday." April 13, 1977.

Reiterman, Tim, and Malcolm Glover. "Who Is Dave Toschi and Why All the Intrigue?" *San Francisco Examiner*, July 12, 1978.

Ressler, Robert K., and Tom Shachtman. *Whoever Fights Monsters: My Twenty Years Tracking Serial Killers for the FBI.* New York: St. Martin's Press, 1992.

Rubenstein, Steve. "CB Patrol Protects S.F. Gays." *San Francisco Chronicle*, December 24, 1977.

Russell, Ron. "Earl's Last Laugh." *San Francisco Weekly*, February 21, 2007.

Sacramento (CA) Bee. "Arrest Made in Mutilation Slayings." December 15, 1978.

———. "SF Steel Executive Is Shot to Death." December 9, 1976.

Saks, Michael J., et al. "Forensic Bitemark Identification: Weak Foundations, Exaggerated Claims." *Journal of Law and the Biosciences* (2016): 538–75.

San Francisco Chronicle. "A Murder in S.F. Every Other Day." June 2, 1974.

————. "Accused Murderer Hangs Self in Jail." January 19, 1979.

————. "Another Case of Murder, Lands End Muggings." August 14, 1975.

————. "Another Stabbing—At Fox Plaza Sept. 28." October 11, 1975.

————. "Anti-Muggers Keep Busy." 1975.

————. "BAGL Demonstrates at City Hall." February 1975.

————. "Butterflies Continue Patrols, Receive Gifts." December 16, 1976.

————. "Chief Scott's 18 Points for a Safer City." February 11, 1975.

————. "Cops Nab Suspect." March 10, 1977.

————. "Cops Step Up Investigation of Five Frenzy Murders." November 13, 1975.

————. "Doodler Known: Straight Sought in May Gay Slayings." July 14, 1977.

————. "Executive Slain in Home." December 9, 1976.

————. "Gay Pimp Faces 5 Years in Prison." August 6, 1979.

————. "Gays Patrol Streets." December 2, 1976.

————. "Group Forms to Halt Muggings." August 14, 1975.

————. "Hearings Scheduled for Murder Suspects." December 16, 1976.

————. "Identities of Two Slain Men Sought." December 29, 1978.

————. "Insanity Plea by Two in Castration Case." October 11, 1974.

————. "Latest Tenderloin Strangulation Victim Identified." October 11, 1978.

————. "Murder Unsolved." May 22, 1975.

————. "One of Every Three S.F. Murders This Year is Still Unsolved." November 14, 1974.

————. "Parade Draws Over 80,000." July 3, 1975.

————. "Police Checking Doodler Suspect."

————. "Police Investigating Link in 3 Recent Stabbings." July 18, 1974.

————. "Reader Identified Last of Three Victims." August 1, 1974.

————. "San Mateo, Marin Murders May Link." October 12, 1978.

————. "Slain Man Identified." May 14, 1975.

————. "Survivors Frustrate Cops in Multi-Killings." 1977.

————. "Suspect in Executive's Slaying." December 11, 1976.

————. "Suspect Jailed." January 12, 1977.

————. "Suspect Nabbed in Pacific Heights Death." December 10, 1976.

————. "Thugs on Loose in Castro." July 17, 1975.

————. "Torture Murders Strike Again." September 11, 1975.

————. "Two Charged in Polk Street Case." September 8, 1974.

————. "Two Guilty of Castrating Hitchhiker." January 21, 1975.

————. "Two Held in Hitchhiker's Mutilation." September 9, 1974.

————. "Two Held in Tenderloin Murder." December 13, 1976.

————. "Verdicts in Murder Trials." April 7, 1977.

———. "Violence Center Opposed." October 1974.

———. "Witnesses Sought in Beach Killing." January 29, 1974.

Sanders, Prentice Earl, and Bennett Cohen. *Zebra Murders: A Season of Killing, Racial Madness, and Civil Rights.* New York: Hachette, 2006.

Scot, David Cameron. "Letter to the Editor." *Bay Area Reporter*, February 5, 1976.

Sharma, Meher. "The Development of Serial Killers: A Grounded Theory Study." PhD diss., Eastern Illinois University, 2018.

Sharpe, Ivan, and Malcolm Glover. "Gay Community Reacts: 'Afraid, but Strong.'" *San Francisco Examiner*, June 24, 1977.

Spitzer, Robert L. "The Diagnostic Status of Homosexuality in *DSM-III*: A Reformulation of the Issues." *American Journal of Psychiatry* 138, no. 2 (1981): 210–15.

Starr, Kevin. "The City's Supercop." *San Francisco Examiner*, August 13, 1977.

Stewart, Tony. *The Trash Bag Murderer.* Self-published, Lulu Publishing, 2010.

Stryker, Susan, and Jim Van Buskirk. *Gay by the Bay: A History of Queer Culture in the San Francisco Bay Area.* San Francisco: Chronicle Books, 1996.

Times (San Mateo, CA). "Man Suspected of 14 SF Slayings." July 8, 1977.

Vachss, Andrew. "Sex Predators Can't Be Saved." *New York Times*, January 5, 1993.

Van Derbeken, Jaxon. "Man Wrongfully Convicted of Killings to Go Free." *San Francisco Chronicle*, January 12, 2011.

———. "Prosecutors Want Retrial in Double Murder Case." *San Francisco Chronicle*, December 16, 2010.

———. "S.F. Man Wrongly Convicted on False Testimony." *San Francisco Chronicle*, December 15, 2010.

———. "S.F. May Pay Freed Man $4.5 Million Settlement." *San Francisco Chronicle*, June 4, 2009.

Van Dijk, Teun A. "Principles of Critical Discourse Analysis." *Discourse & Society* 4, no. 2 (1993): 249–83.

Venice-Marina News (Santa Monica, CA). "Missing Venice Boy's Body Found in Forest." June 16, 1977.

Verma, Anoop K., Sachil Kumar and Sandeep Bhattacharya. "Identification of a Person with the Help of Bite Mark Analysis." *Journal of Oral Biology and Craniofacial Research* 3, no. 2 (May–August 2013): 88–91.

Watt, Nick. "This Serial Murder Case Has Been Cold for More Than 40 Years. Now Police Say They Have a Suspect." CNN, June 21, 2018.

Weiss, Mike. "New Zodiac Disclosures: Inspector Toschi Talks." *San Francisco Chronicle*, July 14, 1978.

West, Don. "Ex-Con Held in 3 Gay Killings." *San Francisco Examiner*, December 13, 1978.

Wright, Guy. "A Fan Letter for Dave Toschi." *San Francisco Examiner*, July 23, 1978.

Young, William (San Mateo County Sheriff's Office sergeant). Interview with the author, 2021.

Zane, Maitland. "The Gay Killers." *San Francisco Chronicle*, January 20, 1976.

———. "The Sado Murder Horror." *San Francisco Chronicle*, January 19, 1976.

ABOUT THE AUTHOR

Kate Zaliznock is a Bay Area–based writer and editor. Her past work has covered a wide range of topics, including music, history, science, pop culture, and politics. She is also the founder of Open Color, an arts collective and magazine that features both emerging and established artists from around the globe. This is her first book on true crime.